Designing Camelot

Designing Camelot

The Kennedy White House Restoration

James A. Abbott

Elaine M. Rice

VNR Van Nostrand Reinhold
I(T)P® A Division of International Thomson Publishing Inc.

New York • Albany • Bonn • Boston • Detroit • London • Madrid • Melbourne • Mexico City • Paris • San Francisco • Singapore • Tokyo • Toronto

Van Nostrand Reinhold Staff:

Executive Editor: Roberto de Alba

Aquisitions Editor: Jane Degenhardt

Associate Editor: Beth Harrison

Senior Production Editor: Carla Nessler

Production Director: Louise Kurtz

Production Assistant: Kimee Davidson

Marketing Manager: Lis Pearson

Senior Marketing Associate: Karren Abrams

Cover designer: Mike Suh

Text designer: Paul Costello

Copyright © 1998 by Van Nostrand Reinhold

I(T)P® an International Thomson Publishing Company
The ITP logo is a registered trademark used herein under license

Printed in the United States of America

For more information, contact:

Van Nostrand Reinhold
115 Fifth Avenue
New York, NY 10003

Chapman & Hall
2-6 Boundary Row
London
SE1 8HN
United Kingdom

Thomas Nelson Australia
102 Dodds Street
South Melbourne, 3205
Victoria, Australia

Nelson Canada
1120 Birchmount Road
Scarborough, Ontario
Canada M1K 5G4

Chapman & Hall GmbH
Pappelallee 3
69469 Weinheim
Germany

International Thomson Publishing Asia
221 Henderson Road #05-10
Henderson Building
Singapore 0315

International Thomson Publishing Japan
Hirakawacho Kyowa Building, 3F
2-2-1 Hirakawacho
Chiyoda-ku, 102 Tokyo
Japan

International Thomson Editores
Seneca 53
Col. Polanco
11560 Mexico D.F. Mexico

1 2 3 4 5 6 7 8 9 10   RRD-ROA   03 02 01 00 99 98 97

Library of Congress Cataloging-in-Publication Data

Abbott, James A.
    Designing Camelot : The Kennedy White House Restoration

        p.   cm.
    Includes bibliographical references.
    ISBN 0-442-02532-7
        1. Building--American--History.   I. Abbott, James A.   II. Elaine,
    M. Rice.   III. Title.
TH105.F73   1997   97-825
690'.0952—dc21   CIP

www.vnr.com
product discounts • free email newsletters
software demos • online resources

email: info@vnr.com

A service of I(T)P®

PAGE ii: Courtesy CBS Photo Archives.

PAGE viii: John F. Kennedy Library

This book is dedicated to:

My favorite author, CDS; my first White House tour guide, my brother Robert;
and the memory of its inspiration, Mary Anna Davies Starr Abbott (1921-1989)

—J.A.A.

My mother, Bette Schum Rice, who first showed me the White House,
and the memory of my father, Charles Walter Rice (1930-1997)

—E.M.R.

Contents

Foreword

As I look back over the past thirty-plus years, I realize more than ever the importance and lasting influence of the Kennedy Restoration of the White House. It became a model for historic houses all over America as well as for governors' mansions, where many of our states' First Ladies emulated the efforts of Jacqueline Kennedy. The regal and courtly presence of the White House attained during the Kennedy years has been retained during the subsequent presidencies. There is still an active Fine Arts Committee—now known as the Committee for the Preservation of the White House—and an Office of the Curator.

As the second Curator of the White House during the Kennedy Administration, I have read *Designing Camelot* with great interest. It is the result of James A. Abbott's lifelong interest in the restoration and refurbishing of the White House during the Kennedy years. Following his 1995 exhibition, *A Frenchman in Camelot,* this book meticulously documents the role played by French interior designer Stéphane Boudin and his firm, Jansen. It also focuses attention on Henry Francis du Pont, another leading figure in the Kennedy restoration project. Elaine M. Rice, the book's coauthor, became sufficiently interested in this aspect of the restoration as a Winterthur Fellow to choose the accomplishments of du Pont and the Fine Arts Committee as the subject of her thesis. Combining their respective subjects of interest, Mr. Abbott and Ms. Rice have produced a concise history of this publicly admired project, acknowledging the contributions of the numerous participants while documenting the evolution of each room.

The White House has always served as a national symbol. However, at no other time in our history has the "President's House" been associated with quite the same degree of grandeur as that created for President and Mrs. John F. Kennedy. *Designing Camelot* provides an opportunity to explore this famous transformation.

William Voss Elder III

Acknowledgments

This book would not have been possible without the support and encouragement of a number of people. To Mrs. Charles B. Wrightsman we extend gratitude for a generosity that made possible both the 1995 exhibition *A Frenchman in Camelot* and, subsequently, this publication.

It is impossible to recognize every participant in the Kennedy-era restoration of the White House, but we do wish to thank several who have shared their recollections and assisted in this written record of the project. John A. H. Sweeney, Curator Emeritus of Winterthur, has generously shared his recollections of Henry F. du Pont as well as his own remembrances of the White House project. William Voss Elder III has also described his experiences as Curator of the White House. We are equally indebted to Paul Manno for his sharing of information regarding the work of Jansen and Stéphane Boudin for President and Mrs. Kennedy. We also wish to thank Arthur Kouwenhoven, Lorraine Waxman Pearce, James Ketchum, Albert Hadley, Edwin and Adriana Bitter, Janet Felton Cooper, and Clement Conger for their various contributions.

Outside of the participants, we acknowledge the invaluable help of archivist Allan B. Goodrich and Curator Frank Rigg of the John F. Kennedy Library; Curator Betty Monkman and Associate Curator William Allman of the White House; archivist Heather Clewell and librarian Neville Thompson at Winterthur; James C. Curtis of the University of Delaware; Curators Charles Hind and Andrew Norris of the British Architectural Library, Royal Institute of British Architects; Winfred Dohl and Nina Silberstein of David Webb; Mimi Calver and Edward Papenfuse of the Maryland State Archives; Nancy Porter of Parish-Hadley; Nancy Press of The Baltimore Museum of Art; Scalamandré; Ruth Lord; William Seale; Carol Prisant; Mark Hampton; Joseph T. Butler; Mary Jane Pool; Jim Frank; Rachelle and Jonathan Schneider; Khushrow Press; Claude D'Costa; Svenja Soldovieri; M. B. Munford; and Mary Fagan. We also wish to acknowledge Lindley Kirksey, Roberto de Alba, and the staff of Van Nostrand Reinhold.

A special thank-you is due architect Robert Bentley Adams, whose life-long interest in the White House made him a valuable source of information as well as a supportive critic. His time and talent have been greatly appreciated.

J.A.A. and E.M.R.

CHAPTER ONE

The Kennedy Style

From the moment President John F. Kennedy took the oath of office, his administration was characterized as having *style*. Even prior to that cold January day in 1961, there was a sense that the young president-elect and his beautiful wife, Jacqueline, were bringing to the White House a new vigor and glamour. The Kennedy image was more than one of style and wealth—it was an image of sophisticated youth, of a younger generation that embodied the country's future, yet appreciated the glory of its past. When the poet Robert Frost read his poem "The Gift Outright," composed especially for the inaugural, it was the beginning of what one author of the time called "a cultural renaissance in America."[1]

President Kennedy surrounded himself with prestigiously educated, artistic, and cultivated people. Popular literature and newspapers made repeated references to his illustrious cabinet and advisors, nicknamed "the Brain Trust," which consisted of sixteen Rhodes scholars as well as artists, collectors, and authors. Their accessibility, and that of the President, was a welcome surprise to the media, who often found themselves poolside or sharing the putting green with the nation's leaders and administration insiders. Many of the President's extended family of siblings and their spouses became prominent players in his administration and soon became the social stars of Washington. But, most important, at his side was a wife who was immediately perceived to have a style unto herself that eclipsed that of any of her contemporaries.

LEFT: *The State dinner at Mount Vernon, held in honor of the visit of the President of Pakistan, Mohammed Ayub Khan, in July 1961, was the first of its kind held outside the White House. Here, President and Mrs. Kennedy pose on the lawn with their guest of honor, accompanied by his daughter, the Begum Nasir Aurangzeb. Jacqueline Kennedy is wearing one of the dresses created for her by Oleg Cassini. She is said to have requested that the dress be columnar in shape to echo Mount Vernon's historic façade. Courtesy John F. Kennedy Library.*

Jacqueline Bouvier Kennedy quickly captured the imagination of the country with her beauty, grace, and intelligence. She was the most written-about, talked-about, and photographed woman of her day. "Much too sophisticated in her tastes to be typical," as one author put it, the First Lady nevertheless became a cultural icon and role model to many American women.[2] Department-store mannequins assumed her likeness, ladies' heads across the country were coiffed with her characteristic bouffant bob, and newspaper articles featured details of her wardrobe after every public appearance. Jacqueline Kennedy presented the picture of a devoted wife and mother who could also circulate among the world's leaders with the skill of a veteran diplomat.

With this youthful and energetic couple at the reins of power, Washington, D.C., took on a new air of elegance and excitement. Suddenly the White House was filled with Shakespearean actors, classical ballerinas, and world-class musicians. Glamorous state dinners where movie stars mingled with poets were followed by dancing, with President and Mrs. Kennedy leading the floor. "The New Frontier" being charted by the youngest elected President in this country's history evoked images of a grand past. As Robert

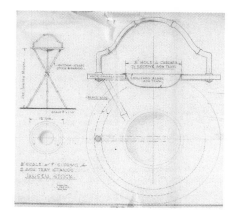

LEFT: *This crèche was part of the Kennedys' 1962 Christmas display in the East Room. It was lent and arranged by Mrs. Howell Howard of New York, a collector of seventeenth- and eighteenth-century nativity figures. It was placed in front of a velvet backdrop and framed by the room's gold brocade curtains. Courtesy John F. Kennedy Library.*

ABOVE: *Design for a portable standing ashtray to be used in the East Room following State dinners. Designed by Jansen's New York Office following Jacqueline Kennedy's personal specifications. Two of these ashtrays were produced for the White House. Courtesy Paul Manno. Photo: Jim Frank.*

Frost characterized it, the Kennedy administration promised to be ". . . a next Augustan age . . . a golden age of poetry and power, of which this noonday's the beginning hour."[3] The image of the Presidency underwent a metamorphosis as the stately yet staid era of the Eisenhowers ended and the excitement of the Kennedy administration began.

The power of imagery was well understood by Jack Kennedy. He had grown up in a family whose image was carefully fostered by its patriarch, Joseph P. Kennedy. From the time of his youth, President Kennedy was made aware of the importance of the media in shaping one's public presence. To the father obsessed with social and political success, his son's gaining the presidency realized the height of his aspirations. Joseph Kennedy recognized the beautiful and sophisticated Jacqueline Bouvier to be a valuable asset to his son. Despite her disdain for politics she dutifully accompanied her husband through the campaigns that culminated in his run for the Presidency in 1960. Upon his victory she entered the national spotlight—where she remained for the rest of her life.

America's new First Lady immediately focused her attention on the White House, an interest that was rooted in her youth. She recalled feeling somewhat let down upon her first visit to the mansion, at age eleven. As she told *Life* magazine's Hugh Sidey in 1961, "From the outside I remember the feeling of the place. But inside, all I remember is shuffling through. There wasn't even a booklet you could buy. Mount Vernon and the National Gallery of Art made a far greater impression."[4] From the moment she knew her husband was planning to run for the Presidency, she felt that the White House would be one of her main projects if he won. A First Lady interested in the appearance of the White House was not new; however, her efforts far surpassed the predictable new draperies, fresh paint, and reupholstering that previous residents had contributed.

With Jacqueline Kennedy as its chatelaine, the White House became the stage on which the drama of the Kennedy administration was played. Beyond the transformation of the rooms of the house, she and her husband endeavored to enhance the entire atmosphere surrounding the Presidency. They strove for excellence—an excellence in all facets of life at the White House, from dining and entertainment to decoration and diplomacy. Each aspect was guided by an aesthetic carefully and skillfully created, if not by the

BELOW: *Excerpts from Mozart's* Magic Flute *were performed by the Opera Society of Washington for the visit of President Radhakrishnan of India on June 3, 1963. Here, the dramatic scene as Sarastro sings to Pamina is set against the velvet backdrop of the portable stage in the East Room. Courtesy John F. Kennedy Library.*

Kennedys themselves, then with the assistance of the talented friends and advisors who circulated around the first couple.

The quality and style of entertaining at the White House changed dramatically during the Kennedy administration. For the first time, cocktails were served and smoking was allowed in the State Rooms. Receiving lines, except for the most formal occasions, were eliminated, as the Kennedys preferred to walk through the rooms casually greeting each of their guests. This relaxed atmosphere was carried over to the State Dining Room, where the traditional E-shaped table arrangement was replaced by more informal round tables. This allowed greater flexibility with regard to protocol, with high-ranking guests being dispersed among the tables, and created a more comfortable environment for socializing. On occasion, tables were also placed in the Blue Room, extending the formal dining area into the State Parlors for the

A typical table setting at a Kennedy State dinner included a centerpiece of informally arranged flowers, dinnerware from one of the recent Presidential services, and vermeil flatware. Jacqueline Kennedy purchased a new set of simple glass stemware manufactured in West Virginia to complement the ornate china and silver. Courtesy John F. Kennedy Library.

first time. All the rooms were decorated with casual Flemish-inspired arrangements of fresh flowers, as opposed to the large, static selections of previous White House occupants. Fireplaces were lit, and candlelight provided the majority of illumination, creating a soft glow throughout the State Rooms.

Prior to the arrival of the Kennedys, dining at the White House was not necessarily distinguished by its culinary excellence. The appointment of French chef René Verdon in the spring of 1961 ushered in a new era of haute cuisine in the White House. Jacqueline Kennedy saw to every detail, selecting menus and detailing their presentation in long, handwritten memos to the staff. At her direction, dinners were shortened from the traditional seven courses to five or fewer, allowing more time for the entertainment that became the focal point of an evening at the Kennedy White House.

The character and quality of entertainment at the Kennedy White House became even more celebrated than the cuisine. The well-known photograph of cellist Pablo Casals performing in the East Room in November 1961 came to symbolize the artistic excellence that President and Mrs. Kennedy sought. Casals's was only one of many spectacular performances staged in the East Room. Employing the same philosophy she applied to the furnishings in the executive mansion, Jacqueline Kennedy believed that any performer in the White House should be the best that the country had to

LEFT: *President and Mrs. Kennedy approach the portable stage in the East Room to congratulate mezzo-soprano Grace Bumbry after her concert on February 20, 1962. It was the first major appearance in the United States for the American-born singer, who had already achieved fame in Europe. The Kennedys sought to enhance her fame in her own country by inviting her to perform in the White House. Courtesy John F. Kennedy Library.*

BELOW: *The arrival on the South Lawn of Premier Ben Bella of Algeria on October 15, 1962, marked the first time an official welcoming ceremony was held on the grounds of the White House rather than at one of Washington's airports or at Union Station. Mrs. Kennedy, holding her son John F. Kennedy, Jr., can be seen unofficially viewing the ceremony near the left of the photo. Courtesy John F. Kennedy Library.*

offer. A portable stage, hung with a velvet backdrop, was specially created for the East Room, transforming the elegant space into a theater suitable for a variety of talent. Shakespearean plays, classical ballet, contemporary vocalists, and many other performances provided the finale to evenings of casually elegant and intellectually stimulating entertainment at the White House.

The Kennedys turned their attention to the grounds of the White House as well. The Rose Garden, once a nondescript patch of hedge-rowed lawn, was transformed by the Kennedys' friend Mrs. Paul Mellon. Rachel Lambert ("Bunny") Mellon did not have any formal landscape training when she was asked to help at the White House. However, her vision of a tree-lined outdoor receiving area complemented the Kennedys' sense of ceremony and their affinity for informal settings. The President took a special interest in this space, suggesting the placement of steps from the outside colonnade of the White House to the lawn. If the White House interiors were a figurative stage for the Kennedys, this entrance to the Rose Garden was a literal one, where the president and his guests of honor could stand elevated before the assembly in a stately outdoor setting.

The visits of foreign dignitaries became events of high ceremony during the Kennedy administration. An arriving head of state might expect to be greet-

ABOVE: *These paperweights were designed by David Webb, the prestigious New York jeweler, following the directive of Jacqueline Kennedy. The one at left, made of brilliant blue stone and decorated with gold and turquoise, was designed for the Grand Duchess Charlotte of Luxembourg who visited Washington in April 1963. At right is the gift presented to Chancellor Adenauer of West Germany, made of iron ore and gold roping. Courtesy David Webb Jewelers. Photo: Jim Frank.*

ABOVE RIGHT: *Air Force One, the official airplane of the President, shown here on November 10, 1962. American industrial designer Raymond Loewy designed both the exterior paint treatment and the interior decoration of the plane for President Kennedy, who was the first American President of the Jet Age. He often used the plane for in-flight meetings with members of his cabinet and the press. Courtesy John F. Kennedy Library.*

ed on the South Lawn by a full honor guard composed, for the first time, of representatives of all four branches of the military, followed by a lavish state dinner. The most extravagant of these dinners was held for the president of Pakistan at Mount Vernon, the home of George Washington. This event marked the first time a state dinner was held outside the White House at a historic house and epitomized the sense of history and grandeur for which the Kennedys were renowned. Even the traditional parting gifts presented to visiting officials were made more special by the Kennedys. After visiting the mineral and gem exhibition at the Smithsonian Institution, Jacqueline Kennedy was inspired to commission David Webb, the New York jeweler, to create paperweights made of minerals native to America, mounted in gold. A presentation inscription was personalized for each recipient of these exotic and original gifts.

With a new generation in power, led by the charismatic President and his wife, the city of Washington itself began to reflect a more cosmopolitan attitude. Considered a cultural wasteland, the nation's capital began to sponsor more artistic and cultural activities. From very grand projects, such as the proposal for a National Cultural Center, to the simple introduction of European-style sidewalk cafés, Washington, D.C., acquired an air of sophistication that reflected the interests of its most famous pair of residents.

Jacqueline Kennedy viewing the model of the proposed renovations to Lafayette Square townhouses located directly across from the White House, on October 17, 1962. President Kennedy, strongly supported by Mrs. Kennedy, prevented the demolition of these historic homes by overriding legislation to raze them to make way for a federal office building. To the right of Mrs. Kennedy is the architect in charge of the Lafayette Square restoration, John Carl Warnecke, who later designed President Kennedy's grave at Arlington Cemetery. Courtesy John F. Kennedy Library.

The city of Washington particularly benefited from the Kennedys' interest in cultural enhancement and the arts. President and Mrs. Kennedy worked in conjunction with the French minister of culture, André Malraux, to have Leonardo da Vinci's *Mona Lisa* exhibited at the National Gallery of Art in January 1963. The row of historic townhouses in Lafayette Park, across from the White House, was saved from destruction by Mrs. Kennedy's personal interest in its preservation. And the National Cultural Center, initially proposed during the Eisenhower administration, was strongly supported by President Kennedy, who oversaw the early development of the Washington arts center that was eventually named in his honor. The Kennedys' support of American performing artists, so many of whom were invited to perform in the White House, increased public awareness of the arts in the capital and throughout the country.

President Kennedy inspects a model for the proposed
National Cultural Center in the State Dining
Room in August 1963. With him are members of
the committee for the building of the center, including
its architect, Edward Durrel Stone, who stands to
the President's left. Eventually this building became
the John F. Kennedy Center for the Performing Arts.
Courtesy John F. Kennedy Library.

The pervasiveness of their interests and the range of their influence can
still be felt today. However, nowhere was the Kennedy style more evident
than in the rooms in which they lived and worked in the White House
between 1961 and 1963. Far beyond the mere selection of furniture and fabrics, the interiors of the White House reflected the desire of the Kennedys,
and Jacqueline Kennedy in particular, to associate themselves with a grand
historical past. The leaders of "The New Frontier" chose to surround themselves with images of the past. The White House became the ultimate theater

The Lincoln Continental used by President Kennedy from May 1961, when it was delivered, until his assassination in November 1963. It was the first Presidential limousine to be painted navy blue rather than black. This blue limousine evoked a more youthful and sophisticated image and was another of the subtle yet stylish accents to the Kennedy presidency. Courtesy John F. Kennedy Library.

in which to stage this nation's continued history—not only for the American audience but for the world as a whole. Like the founding fathers who sought to refine the young and unsophisticated United States, the Kennedys sought to remind the nation of those early efforts and to define themselves as the rightful heirs to that legacy. The restoration of the White House during the Kennedy administration dramatized the power of personalities and the power of images to define societies both past and present—a drama played out on the stage of the ultimate historic American house.

Restoration: Idea and Organization

LEFT: *In conjunction with the work of the Fine Arts Committee, a special Paintings Committee was formed by Mrs. Kennedy. Some of its members are photographed here in the Green Room, along with Mrs. Kennedy and Henry du Pont, following a tea given in their honor on December 5, 1961. Seated, left to right Mrs. Kennedy; Mr. James Fosburgh, Chairman of the Paintings Committee; Mrs. Joseph Alsop. Standing, left to right Mrs. Suzette M. Zurcher; Mr. Stanley Marcus; Mr. Lawrence Fleischmann; Mrs. James Fosburgh; Mr. Nathaniel Saltonstall; Mrs. J. Cheever; Mr. du Pont; Mrs. Walter Halle; Mrs. William Paley; and Mr. Joseph Pulitzer, Jr. Prior to the formation of this committee, the White House collection consisted almost exclusively of portraiture, much of which was of mediocre quality. As a result of the Committee's work, several original portraits of presidents were acquired, along with many fine eighteenth- and nineteenth-century paintings. Courtesy John F. Kennedy Library.*

On February 23, 1961, Jacqueline Kennedy launched the most historic and celebrated redecoration of the White House in its history. The White House announced Mrs. Kennedy's plan to locate and buy the finest period furniture, with which the historical integrity of the executive mansion's interiors would be restored. The White House press release issued that day said that a twelve-member committee had been appointed to advise Mrs. Kennedy on the selection of appropriate furnishings and to raise funds to buy pieces targeted by its members. The committee was chaired by Henry Francis du Pont, the multi-millionaire from Wilmington, Delaware, and the premier collector of Americana. Under his guidance, the committee would select only authentic and historically accurate objects that reflected the illustrious history of the White House.

The cornerstone of this famous residence was laid in 1792. Designed by James Hoban, the house was first occupied by President John Adams and his wife Abigail in November 1800. Burned by the British in 1814 during the War of 1812, much of the original interior architecture and furnishings were destroyed or otherwise lost. In the years following its reconstruction, the Executive Mansion was periodically altered, most notably in 1902 when President Theodore Roosevelt hired the New York firm McKim, Mead, & White to refurbish the State Rooms in the contemporary Beaux Arts style. By the late 1940s, during the administration of President Harry Truman, the structure of the house was determined to be dangerously fragile and a dra-

News of Mrs. Kennedy's restoration project was carried throughout the country in press announcements describing her plans for the White House and the formation of the Fine Arts Committee. The plea for antique furnishings of the early nineteenth century, particularly those related to the history of the White House, resulted in a landslide of mail to Mrs. Kennedy and to Henry du Pont from people offering to sell or donate family heirlooms. Authors' collection.

matic interior reconstruction was undertaken. The Truman family moved across the street to Blair House while the White House was literally gutted, leaving only the exterior walls intact. With new walls and floors installed in the original configuration, the interior woodwork was returned to the rooms, now structurally sound, but lacking any real decorative cohesion. This was the house that President and Mrs. Kennedy moved into and were determined to improve.

Jacqueline Kennedy was not the first First Lady to attempt a historical approach. In 1924 Grace Coolidge, wife of President Calvin Coolidge, appointed an official committee of advisors to the White House to select historical furnishings for the public rooms. The committee was composed largely of wealthy patrons of the arts, several of whom supervised the installation of the American Wing in the Metropolitan Museum of Art earlier that year that sparked a sensation for early American design among antiques enthusiasts. In both aesthetics and methodology, the Coolidge refurnishing anticipated the Kennedy restoration. Like Jacqueline Kennedy, Grace Coolidge envisioned a historical redecoration featuring Colonial American style. The project went awry when a major controversy developed between two factions within the project: antiquarians wanting to obliterate any reference to pre–World War I imperialism and restore the rooms to Colonial simplicity and architects wanting to preserve the integrity of the Beaux-Arts interiors that had been installed at the turn of the century. The very public quarreling among the advisors caused a media frenzy and, in the end, President Coolidge ordered a halt to the project. When a more discreet committee resumed the work two years later, the result was the successful completion of the Green Room as a Federal-style parlor.[1]

The Coolidge restoration, although it fell short of the dramatic effect its organizers had hoped for, set several important precedents. The White House was elevated in public perception to a status beyond current fashion trends, worthy of protection from the personal whims of Presidents and First Ladies. The emphasis on historical integrity led to the establishment of the "period room" concept in the White House—an idea interpreted and molded by a long succession of First Ladies to come. Also, the method of working within a committee structure to decorate the White House was adopted. The culmination of the effort was the first congressional action recognizing the permanent value of the White House interiors. In February 1925 Congress passed a joint resolution permitting the White House to accept gifts of furniture and artwork. It also increased the annual appropriation of funds for interior maintenance and refurbishing from $20,000 to $50,000.

In the early 1930s Lou Hoover, wife of President Herbert Hoover, sponsored the first serious research into original White House furnishings by attempting to document the history of each object in the house. As Jacqueline Kennedy did years later, Mrs. Hoover combed the basement and storerooms to find treasures for the new "historic" interiors. Reproductions were mingled among originals to create period settings. In 1960 Mamie Eisenhower, wife of President Dwight Eisenhower, sponsored the redecoration of the Diplomatic Reception Room as a Federal-style parlor. J. B. West, chief usher of the White House from 1941 to 1969, recalled in his memoirs that Mrs. Eisenhower wanted to refurnish the entire house with antiques but, due to the recent structural renovation during the Truman administration, the furnishings appropriation from Congress had been revoked. She had to settle for redecorating the family quarters, leaving the "B. Altman" White House and the infamous "Mamie pink" to her successor. Likewise, although President Truman wanted antiques for the State rooms, all funds in his administration were limited to the renovation.

It did not take Jacqueline Kennedy long to hide the signature pastel of her predecessor under new slipcovers and upholstery and to remove the department-store furniture that dominated the family quarters. Within weeks of President Kennedy's inauguration the well-known society decorator Mrs. Henry Parish II, or "Sister," as she was known, was at work transforming the rooms with the chintz-laden, casually elegant style that was the hallmark of her New York firm. In two weeks' time the entire appropriation of $50,000 for improvement to the White House had been spent on the private quarters alone. But Jacqueline Kennedy, undaunted in her zeal to refurnish the rest of the house, told J. B. West, "I know we're out of money . . . but never mind . . . we're going to find some way to get real antiques into this house."[2]

Jacqueline Kennedy did not have to look far to find a solution to her decorating dilemma. According to John Sweeney, at the time Curator at Winterthur, Henry du Pont's estate-turned-museum outside Wilmington, Delaware, Mrs. Kennedy's initial plan was to request a loan of antique fur-

ABOVE: *John Sweeney, Curator of the Winterthur Museum, guides Jacqueline Kennedy through the museum on her visit in May 1961. Mrs. Kennedy sought inspiration for the restored rooms of the White House from the work of her chairman, Henry du Pont. Few photographs exist of her visit, as du Pont prohibited press photographers from entering the estate, saying that he couldn't understand why such a fuss was being made about him having a guest for lunch. Courtesy Winterthur Museum.*

FACING PAGE: *In this portrait by Aaron Shikler, painted in 1965, Henry Francis du Pont is shown in the conservatory of his home on the estate at Winterthur. After the opening of his original home as the Winterthur Museum in 1951, du Pont and his wife Ruth moved into this house adjacent to the main building and furnished it with their collection of European decorative arts. Courtesy Winterthur Museum.*

nishings from the museum to the White House. Sweeney, now Curator Emeritus of Winterthur, worked closely with du Pont on the White House project. He recalls that Mrs. Kennedy inquired through a relative who served on the museum's board of trustees about the possibility of Winterthur lending objects from its collection for use in the White House. Charles Montgomery, director of the museum from 1954 to 1961, suggested the alternative solution of appointing Henry du Pont chairman of a committee of informed people to acquire authentic furnishings for the White House. Mrs. Kennedy may not have been able to borrow his furniture, but she could borrow du Pont himself—his expertise and his connections. In her book *Jacqueline Kennedy: The White House Years* Mary Van Rensselaer Thayer states that it was the Kennedys' friend and Fine Arts Committee member Jayne Wrightsman who suggested that Henry du Pont be brought into the project. Ms. Wrightsman and her husband, oil magnate Charles B. Wrightsman, had been long acquainted with the famous collector and were able to arrange a meeting between Mrs. Kennedy and du Pont. No matter how the initial contact was made, there can be little doubt that Henry du Pont was expected by all concerned to be an asset to the restoration and a key to its ultimate success.[3]

A member of one of the wealthiest families in America, Henry Francis du Pont devoted the majority of his life to developing the house and grounds that comprised his estate at Winterthur. Educated in horticulture at Harvard, he directed the operations of a dairy farm on the property and planned the creation of extensive gardens throughout the nine hundred–plus acres. The house, originally built in 1839, was expanded at the turn of the century by du Pont's father, Henry Algernon du Pont. In the 1920s and 1930s, after Henry Francis took ownership, the house was altered to reflect his appreciation for early American design and to accommodate his growing collection of American antiques. When du Pont opened his house at Winterthur to the public as a museum in 1951, after adding a wing of nine stories and nearly two hundred period rooms, he had been collecting American antiques for over twenty years. In the early 1930s, during the height of the Colonial Revival movement, he began incorporating his collection into period rooms, installing architectural woodwork from early American houses as a backdrop for furnishings of the same period. By the time of his association with Mrs. Kennedy and the White House project he was regarded as the greatest collec-

tor of Americana and the highest-qualified authority on the subject of American historical decoration.[4]

Henry du Pont's design aesthetic was based on balance and color harmony achieved through the arrangement of furniture and the selection of upholstery. His enthusiasm for color balance extended out-of-doors to the garden, where he directed the planting of flowers of complementary colors to be seen through the windows of rooms at varying seasons. Despite the many spectacular pieces in his collection, du Pont believed that no single item should dominate any room. This philosophy was summed up in his oft-quoted phrase, "If you go into a room, and right away see something, then you realize that that [something] shouldn't be in the room."[5]

The product of du Pont's philosophy often had less to do with historical authenticity and more to do with an antiquarian's vision of a grand and ordered past. However, in the years preceding 1961 he had begun to style himself as an academic-minded collector, paying closer attention to historical design documents and social history-based evidence. His commitment to scholarship manifested itself in the establishment of the Winterthur Program in Early American Culture in 1952, the first graduate program devoted to the study of American decorative arts, and the 1964 launching of *Winterthur Portfolio,* a scholarly publication featuring new research in material culture. Winterthur became the foremost research institution for American decorative arts, and Henry du Pont emerged not only as a collector but also as an educator. Du Pont was widely acclaimed for his efforts and received, among many other awards, honorary doctoral degrees from Yale, Williams, and the University of Delaware. The year he was appointed chairman of the Fine Arts Committee he received the Louise du Pont Crowninshield Award (named for his sister) by the National Trust for Historical Preservation. He served as a trustee of several museums and botanical organizations and was a member of many cultural groups, among them the American Antiquarian Society, the American Philosophical Society, and the Walpole Society. By enlisting him in the White House project, Jacqueline Kennedy fulfilled two critical requirements for success: historical and artistic legitimacy in the public's eyes, and the support of a very powerful network of dealers and collectors in the field of American antiques.

Jacqueline Kennedy herself had access to the wealthiest and most socially prominent people in American society. Between her own connections and those of her husband's family, Mrs. Kennedy was acquainted with many of the country's most affluent individuals. Some of these friends became members of the Fine Arts Committee, including Jayne Wrightsman, who with her husband Charles, had assembled an important collection of eighteenth-century French furniture and, in so doing, had become familiar with antique dealers and collectors throughout Europe. These contacts, particularly with the Parisian firm Maison Jansen, proved very helpful in acquiring furnishings for the White House. Other members of the committee were Gerald Shea, who had helped to assemble Joseph P. Kennedy's antiques collection in Hyannisport, and Jane Engelhard, a New York socialite and member of the International Council of the Museum of Modern Art.

In appointing the Fine Arts Committee, Mrs. Kennedy and du Pont pooled their personal resources and assembled a formidable group of people who could make the restoration a reality.

FINE ARTS COMMITTEE FOR THE WHITE HOUSE
Chairman: Mr. Henry F. du Pont
Honorary Chairman: Mrs. John F. Kennedy
Mr. Charles Francis Adams
Mrs. C. Douglas Dillon
Mrs. Charles W. Engelhard
Mr. David E. Finley
Mrs. Albert D. Lasker
Mr. John S. Loeb
Mrs. Paul Mellon
Mrs. Henry Parish II
Mr. Gerald Shea
Mr. John Walker III
Mrs. George Henry Warren
Mrs. Charles B. Wrightsman

While some of the members were museum professionals, most were antiques enthusiasts without any formal training in objects connoisseurship. More important to the White House project than formal training, however, were wealth and connections—and these qualities were abundant among the group. It was assumed that these twelve influential people, through their network of affluent friends, would find donors of money and furnishings to the project, alleviating the need to petition Congress for more appropriations.

To augment the status of the Fine Arts Committee and to further promote the image of the restoration as an academic endeavor, an Advisory Committee was appointed, also under the chairmanship of Henry du Pont. In a letter to Mrs. Kennedy, du Pont listed his choices for advisors and outlined his priorities in making selections: "First, to find those whose training and present positions equip them to supplement the knowledge and experience of the members of our committee; second, to assure nationwide representation; and third, to include those working in the following areas of research into our country's past—the fine arts, the decorative arts, and cultural history."[6]

FINE ARTS ADVISORY COMMITTEE

Mr. James Biddle, *Assistant Curator in Charge of the American Wing,*
The Metropolitan Museum of Art

Dr. Julian P. Boyd, *Editor,* The Jefferson Papers, Princeton University

Dr. Lyman H. Butterfield, *Editor,* The Adams Papers,
Massachusetts Historical Society

Dr. Richard E. Fuller, *President and Director,* The Seattle Art Museum

Mr. Gerald G. Gibson, *Assistant Curator of Decorative Arts,*
Henry Ford Museum

Mr. John M. Graham II, *Director and Curator of Collections,*
Colonial Williamsburg

Mr. Calvin S. Hathaway, *Director,* The Cooper Union Museum

Miss Ima Hogg, *Founder and Curator,* Bayou Bend Collection

Mr. Thomas C. Howe, *Director,*
The California Palace of the Legion of Honor

Dr. Sherman E. Lee, *Director,* Cleveland Museum of Art

Mr. Jack R. McGregor, *Administrative Assistant,*
The Metropolitan Museum of Art

Mr. Henry P. McIlhenny, *Curator of Decorative Arts,*
Philadelphia Museum of Art

Mr. Charles Nagel, *Director,* City Art Museum of St. Louis

Mr. Richard H. Randall, Jr., *Assistant Curator,*
Museum of Fine Arts, Boston

Dr. Edgar P. Richardson, *Director,* The Detroit Institute of Arts

Mr. Marvin D. Schwartz, *Curator of Decorative Arts,* The Brooklyn Museum

Mr. John A. H. Sweeney, *Curator,*
The Henry Francis du Pont Winterthur Museum

Mr. C. Malcolm Watkins, *Curator,* Division of Cultural History,
Smithsonian Institution

Most of the eighteen members of the Advisory Committee were museum professionals or academicians. Beyond national representation, their geographic locations were selected in order to provide a regional representative to inspect items for acquisition that were inaccessible to the East Coast-based Fine Arts Committee. Of this group of advisors, John Sweeney was the most active, serving as an agent for du Pont and the Winterthur Museum. Du Pont, in creating this Advisory Committee to work in conjunction with the initial group, developed a network of knowledgeable professionals and collectors who knew how and where to obtain high-quality pieces; he also hoped to set up a structure within which Mrs. Kennedy could enact her plans beyond reproach of the press. He stated his goals for the restoration in the same letter to Mrs. Kennedy, saying he hoped that together these two committees would "achieve your desire of making the White House a symbol of cultural as well as political leadership . . . believing as we do that an understanding of America's cultural past is a prerequisite to a real understanding of our country today, we shall strive to obtain those tangible evidences of the skill of the early craftsman and the taste of his patron which will make the White House . . . an historic document of cultural life in the United States."[7]

The First Lady was keenly aware of the precautions necessary for smooth enactment of her plans. As always, *Life* magazine was there to put the Kennedys and, in particular, Jacqueline Kennedy's project, into the best light possible. Mrs. Kennedy personally oversaw the preparation of a fully illustrated article outlining her plans for the White House that ran in September 1961. In the interview with Hugh Sidey she labeled for posterity her project as a "restoration" and not a mere "redecoration." She confidently stated, "Everything in the White House must have a reason for being there. It would be sacrilege merely to redecorate it—a word I hate. It must be restored, and that has nothing to do with decoration. That is a question of scholarship."[8]

In the first months of his appointment, Henry du Pont asked several historical consultants to draft a statement of philosophy to guide the restoration. In April 1961 two members of the Advisory Committee, Lyman Butterfield, editor of the John Adams Papers, and Julian Boyd, editor of the Thomas Jefferson Papers, submitted a joint treatise entitled "The White House as a Symbol" that outlined the controlling principles for the restoration. The first of these principles emphasized the evolving nature of the White House and the importance of not limiting its interpretation to a single period of occupancy by focusing on a solitary decorative style in the interiors. Second, in relation to the "living" character of the White House, the authors stressed the necessity of being "eclectic" in making furnishing choices representative of a variety of administrations. Third, the authors specifically discussed the Library and the importance of the books housed therein. "Better than most furnishings," they argued, "books can perform both functional and symbolic roles, and the mingling of books of different periods violates no canons of taste."[9]

The Boyd and Butterfield paper was the catalyst for Mrs. Kennedy to alter her original vision of the restoration as focusing entirely on the period of the earliest occupancy of the White House, 1800. She ultimately agreed that the evolving character of the White House required that the committee not adopt a single style period for their plans. She told one interviewer, "The public should have no fear that we might restore the building to its earliest period, leaving out all that came after, or fill it with French furniture, or hang modern pictures all over it and paint it whatever color we like. The White House belongs to our past and no one who cares about our past would treat it that way."[10] And so, guided by the academic standards put forth by Boyd and Butterfield, Jacqueline Kennedy, Henry du Pont, and the Fine Arts Committee embarked upon the project.

The first official meeting of the committee took place on February 21, 1961, in the Red Room of the White House. Eight members were present, although Henry du Pont, who customarily spent the winter months at his residence in Boca Grande, Florida, did not attend, but arranged to have Jane Engelhard send him a confidential report on the proceedings. At this initial meeting, the committee decided to seek only articles of eighteenth- or nineteenth-century origin. Furthermore, only American-made furnishings were to be placed in the State Rooms, but in the President's private rooms, English and French furniture would be acceptable. The "official rooms" on which the project was focused had long been distinguished among the approximately 132 rooms of the house. These State Rooms, located on the ground floor and the first floor, were the focus of the committee's work. The grand parlors on the first floor, canvases for many earlier redecorations, were the areas of highest priority: the Green Room, the Red Room, and the Blue Room. The State Dining Room and the East Room, at either end of the house, were equally high-profile areas for the committee. On the ground floor, the Diplomatic Reception Room (the traditional meeting place for heads of state), the Library, the China Room, and the Vermeil Room comprised the rest of the State Rooms. One second-floor bedroom known as the Rose Bedroom or Queen's Room, and the Lincoln Bedroom, though not open to the public, have traditionally been considered official rooms due to the frequency with which they are used by visiting dignitaries. The restoration project also encompassed many private rooms of the house and certain areas of the West Wing. During the Kennedy administration, prior to the creation of the Press Room, the West Wing contained recreational areas for the First Family, along with the Oval Office and some administrative offices.

At the first meeting, and through subsequent discussions among the principal players, a system was developed whereby desired furnishings could be identified, located, and acquired. To commence the process, copies of a list of items most necessary for the White House, compiled by Mrs. Kennedy and Sister Parish, were distributed to committee members. Some of the items were replacements of unsuitable furniture presently in the house; others were antiques needed to complete the rooms. The procedure to be followed when a gift was offered was stated as follows: "A picture should be taken of the article and sent, together with at least one recognized expert's opinion of its authenticity, to Mrs. Parish at the New York office, 22 East 69th Street. If a gift is not acceptable, Mr. Finley, of the Fine Arts Commission, will refuse it in the name of our Committee, so as not to offend any friends."[11] The memo

The appointment of Lorraine Waxman Pearce as White House Curator in March 1961 received widespread media attention. The position was unprecedented and served to underscore the academic tone of the restoration project. Only twenty-six years old, a wife and mother, Pearce contributed to the youthful, energetic, and well-educated image of the new crop of White House professionals. Authors' collection.

refers to David Finley, who chaired the Commission of Fine Arts, a government commission charged with supervising the display of art throughout the capitol complex, and which theoretically supervised the activities of related organizations in Washington, D.C. Interestingly, no mention of Henry du Pont is made in relation to the approval of gifts. Rather, Sister Parish, an interior decorator, and not an authority on American antiques, was placed in charge of the selection of suitable objects. Thus, from the very beginning there was ambiguity with regard to who was actually in charge of the restoration, an ambiguity that would plague the project throughout its duration. As for Parish, while her professional contributions in the private rooms are well documented, there is little evidence that she ever played a significant role in the restoration of the State Rooms.

Du Pont's absence from the first meeting of the Fine Arts Committee did not indicate a lack of interest on his part. Just two weeks after this meeting, he and Jacqueline Kennedy met at his residence in Florida to apprise him of developments in the program. In a letter to committee members dated March 11, 1961, she described their meeting and the clarification of several administrative issues. She was clearly striving to make du Pont, and the rest of the committee, aware that he was being closely consulted on all matters. To underscore this point, Mrs. Kennedy stated that du Pont alone was authorized to speak on behalf of the committee. Warning of the danger in speaking to the press, she added that, "anything said now, before we have produced results, will only encourage criticism. It is best for all of us to work industriously and privately."[12]

Also at their meeting of March 6, du Pont and Mrs. Kennedy discussed the need for a permanent Curator in the White House to research and organize the growing collection. Mrs. Kennedy preferred to have someone trained in the graduate program at Winterthur; du Pont recommended a former student who he felt would be suitable for the job, Lorraine Waxman Pearce, a 1958 graduate of the Winterthur Program. At Winterthur, Pearce specialized in the French influence on American decorative arts, particularly the work of émigré cabinetmaker Charles-Honoré Lannuier. The announcement of Pearce's appointment as Curator of the White House was made in late March; it was widely written that she was "on loan" from the Smithsonian Institution. However, Lorraine Pearce remembers that she was not formally

The Map Room on the ground floor of the White House served as the first Curator's office. Here, newly acquired items were examined and catalogued by the Curator before being placed in the restored rooms. Courtesy John F. Kennedy Library.

employed by the Smithsonian prior to her appointment and that the affiliation with the Smithsonian was a device for that institution to associate itself with Mrs. Kennedy's project. Other personnel working with the Curator's office included Janet Felton, secretary to the Fine Arts Committee, and William Voss Elder III, hired as registrar of the growing collection of furnishings. William Elder later commented on the role of the Smithsonian in the project, saying that "in the beginning (they) had some connection, I would say the first six months of the restoration program. But after that they had no connection with it at all."[13] The curatorial staff operated from a makeshift office located on the ground floor of the White House that served as a sort of staging area for assessing newly acquired items.

The transformation taking place within the White House was officially sanctioned by Congress when, in September 1961, it expanded upon legislation created nearly a half century earlier in response to Grace Coolidge's restoration efforts. Public Law 87-286 officially declared the White House a museum, stating, in part:

> Articles of furniture, fixtures, and decorative objects of the White House, when declared by the President to be of historic or artistic interest, together with such similar articles, fixtures, and objects as are acquired by the White House in the future when similarly so declared, shall thereafter be considered to be inalienable and the property of the White House. Any such article, fixture, object when not in use or on display in the White House shall be transferred by direction of the President as a loan to the Smithsonian Institution for its care, study, and storage or exhibition, and such articles, fixtures, and objects shall be returned to the White House from the Smithsonian Institution on notice by the President.[14]

The passage of this act allowed the Fine Arts Committee and the Curator's office to assure potential donors that their gift to the White House would not end up at public auction or in the private collection of a future president. Furthermore, the act protected the historical integrity of the White House by guarding against the possibility of a future administration radically altering the interior decoration of the State Rooms, declaring that ". . . primary attention shall be given to the preservation and interpretation of the museum character of the principal corridor on the ground floor and the principal public rooms on the first floor of the White House."

With this legislation the institutionalization of the White House was official and the work of the Fine Arts Committee in creating period interiors was acknowledged as not only redecoration but historic preservation. Supported by this legislation, Mrs. Kennedy and the staff of the Curator's office began to streamline the White House collection. Department-store reproductions were replaced by long-forgotten treasures dug out of storerooms and warehouses, and the hunt for antiques of appropriate period and origin across the country began in earnest.

The search for antiques for the White House received a great deal of media attention, and before long offers were pouring in from across the United States from people wanting to donate their family heirlooms to the

project. More often than not, these heirlooms proved to be far more personally than historically valuable. However, an occasional gem did descend from someone's attic. At Winterthur, Henry du Pont received hundreds of letters from people offering items for sale or donation to the White House. Each letter was responded to with either a polite decline, a request for further information, or the titillating message that "your letter is being sent on to Mrs. Kennedy for her perusal." In the event that an object was accepted, the donor received a certificate of acknowledgment from the National Park Service, and his or her name was recorded with a description of the object in the catalogue of the collection.

A far more successful method of acquiring objects was through solicitation for donations of items already spotted by Mrs. Kennedy or a member

Mrs. Kennedy's call for antiques for the White House resulted in hundreds of offers for contributions from the public, including this matched pair of antique candy jars, ca. 1860, presented by the Candy, Chocolate, and Confectionary Institute in October 1961. Shown is Letitia Baldridge (r), Mrs. Kennedy's social secretary, accepting the gift from Miss Lea Gallic, who, according to the press release from the National Candy Wholesalers Association, was the "ambassadress for the entire candy industry, touring 60 cities on behalf of the industry." Attentive to period detail, the jars were filled with candy of the type popular in the late nineteenth century. Courtesy John F. Kennedy Library.

of the Fine Arts Committee. Prospective donors, usually acquaintances of committee members, were sent a letter explaining the restoration project and requesting gifts of furniture or funds. A list of desirable objects was sent along with the letter, including approximate prices in order to facilitate their purchase. The hope was that a donor would offer to underwrite the purchase of a specific item. The item would then be listed as the donation of that person, often without the donor ever having seen his or her gift. Although some undesignated monetary donations were made, the majority of donors preferred to have their name associated with a tangible object in the White House collection. The project created a boom for dealers in American antiques. It soon became a status symbol among them to be "in the know" as to what items Mrs. Kennedy and her committee were seeking.

LEFT: *The threat to publicly displayed antiques such as those in the White House is vividly illustrated by this photograph of the Red Room taken on November 5, 1963. A visitor to the White House hurled a decorative urn at a girandole mirror on the south wall, resulting in its near destruction. Most of the wear on White House furnishings was not this severe; however, the incident is indicative of the perils facing a public collection. Courtesy John F. Kennedy Library.*

RIGHT: *In addition to the Curator's office, the ground floor housed a temporary upholsterer's shop, where many of the newly acquired items were repaired and reupholstered. The constant use of White House furnishings resulted in their regular wear and tear, making on-site facilities such as this a necessity. Courtesy John F. Kennedy Library.*

As members of the Fine Arts Committee scouted suitable period furnishings, Henry du Pont took an active role in guiding the restoration. His original recommendations for needed furnishings were the result of a walkthrough on April 29, 1961. His transcribed commentary was brief and often cryptic. For each of the public rooms he made suggestions for stylistic changes and additional furniture, balancing historical authenticity with aesthetic appeal. Du Pont planned to incorporate his initial ideas for the White House rooms into a historical framework. Two days after the initial walkthrough, John Sweeney wrote to Lorraine Waxman Pearce asking that any research reports previously compiled on the White House be sent to du Pont, "as he is eager to begin outlining the program for furnishing the White House and wants it to be based firmly on the results of research."[15] At Winterthur, du Pont enlisted the help of the curatorial staff in researching interior design of the period to be interpreted at the White House. Charles Hummel, then Assistant Curator to John Sweeney, remembers conducting general research for the White House project concerning period color schemes, fabrics, and decorative techniques.[16] Like the rooms at Winterthur, du Pont's plans for the White House included the incorporation of color harmony throughout each room, achieved through complementary furniture

upholstery, floor coverings, and wall and window hangings. However, the White House proved to be far less manageable territory than Winterthur, and as the redecoration of the rooms progressed, du Pont's suggestions were combined with those of other advisors to the project, resulting in a collaborative effect in most of the rooms.

The most significant advisor to the White House project, aside from Henry du Pont, was Frenchman Stéphane Boudin, a favorite society decorator of the time whose work was especially admired by Francophile Jacqueline Kennedy. As the principal decorator for the Parisian firm Maison Jansen, Boudin directed the restoration of numerous European palaces, including Josephine Bonaparte's château, Malmaison. Boudin was initially brought into the project by Jayne Wrightsman, who knew him and suggested that he submit his ideas for the White House to Mrs. Kennedy. Jansen's elaborate proposals, incorporating designs from European interiors, deeply impressed Mrs. Kennedy. By 1962 Stéphane Boudin wielded great control over the appearance of the State Rooms as well as the private quarters.

Henry du Pont was not unaware that his authority within the White House was sometimes undermined by Stéphane Boudin. Contrary to the reports of the contemporary press, he knew that Boudin was working in the

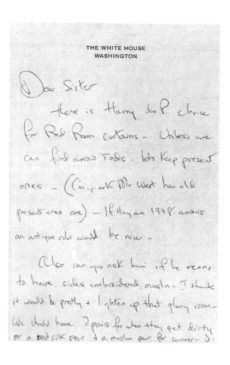

State Rooms and even met with him on rare occasions to review plans and examine furniture. However, du Pont did not feel that Boudin possessed sufficient knowledge of American decorative arts to create historically accurate period settings in the White House, and he frequently disagreed with his ideas. Du Pont's opinion is clearly expressed in a late 1961 letter to Lorraine Waxman Pearce after a meeting with Boudin to look at a suite of French furniture: "I shudder to think what Mr. Boudin would do with American furniture."[17]

The establishment of Lorraine Waxman Pearce as Curator reinforced du Pont's plan to conduct the White House project as an academic endeavor, using the same methodology he used at Winterthur. As a result of her professional training in the Winterthur Program, Pearce regarded du Pont as a mentor, and naturally her loyalty for and veneration of him influenced her work in the White House. Du Pont frequently called her office to give instructions regarding new acquisitions and placement of furniture. She informed him of items being considered for acquisition and solicited his opinion on their suitability. Simultaneously, Pearce received instructions from Mrs. Kennedy that were not always in accord with those of du Pont. This arrangement ultimately put Pearce in a difficult position between two eminent personalities—and two philosophies toward "historical" decoration.

James Bernard West served as Assistant to the Chief Usher of the White House from 1941 to 1957, and as Chief Usher from 1957 through 1969. He was an integral part of Mrs. Kennedy's restoration program, serving as liaison between the various decorators and advisors and as the righthand man to the First Lady. In this photograph taken in May 1962 he is seated in the Entrance Hall on one of the French Empire banquettes placed in that room during the Kennedy restoration. Courtesy John F. Kennedy Library.

Boudin's participation became an increasing source of frustration for Pearce, who viewed him as a threat to the historical accuracy of the rooms that she and du Pont were working to create. "After all of our good work on that famous Tuesday," she wrote to du Pont shortly after the latter's visit in late 1961, "Mr. Boudin arrived fresh and vigorous the next day and promptly undid the Entrance Hall. The two French pier tables were moved around to the Cross Hall, Mrs. [Cornelia] Guest's settee slated for the entrance hall, Miss [Catherine] Bohlen's card table was removed entirely, as were the Lannuier tables, so that the hall is terribly barren and worse than ever. . . . The hall is thus entirely empty of anything but the two pier tables which are out of sight of the entering visitor. I suppose we should keep this entre nous and see if we cannot improve things a bit on your next visit."[18] The discussion of the furnishing of the Entrance Hall that follows will show that, indeed, du Pont's plan was never reincorporated into that space and that Boudin's adjustments remained.

While the curatorial staff of the White House and the Fine Arts Committee members were aware of Boudin's participation, the public was not. Fearing an uproar over a foreign decorator playing a major role in the White House restoration, the Kennedy administration attempted to conceal Boudin's contributions from the press. Despite their efforts, his role was brought to public attention by Maxine Cheshire, a staff reporter for the *Washington Post.* In a series of eight articles titled "Circa 1962: Jacqueline Kennedy's White House," which ran from September 5 through 12, 1962, Cheshire took a critical look at several aspects of the project, including the role of the Fine Arts Committee and that of Stéphane Boudin, claiming to have "raised the velvet curtain" that shrouded the project. Her methods in investigating the articles were less than forthright. As William Elder described, Maxine Cheshire "was out to dig up information and she went to any length to get it."[19] She allegedly used a fake White House identification and press photographer to gain entrance into the studios of such notable players as Jansen and Franco Scalamandré, who headed the New York textile company that provided many of the period reproduction fabrics for the project. These articles, which will be explored in greater detail in following chapters, had the flavor of tabloid journalism as the author uncovered such scandals as the acceptance of a fake desk and the exorbitant price paid for used antique wallpaper. Most important, she exposed the fashionable French decorator who was secretly furnishing America's most historic house.

In one article Cheshire compared Henry du Pont to Stéphane Boudin, stating: "The octogenarian du Pont . . . insists on uncompromising accuracy, right down to getting a music stand and sheet music in the Red Room because it was originally a music room where Dolley Madison's pianoforte and guitar sounded forth for levees. Boudin . . . is an artist whose first concern is visual impact and the creation of an unforgettable architectural effect."[20] Cheshire never interviewed Henry du Pont in preparing her article; therefore, she dealt entirely in the realm of speculation when she concluded that ". . . du Pont claims that Boudin gets carried away."[21]

If the methodologies of du Pont and Boudin represented the opposite ends of the decorating spectrum, then Jacqueline Kennedy's philosophy lay somewhere in between. Like Henry du Pont, she grew up in opulent surroundings and was accustomed to fine furniture. However, her interest in interior decoration was more aesthetic than historical. In her residences Mrs. Kennedy employed decorators to create fashionable interiors that utilized antiques to evoke a feeling of the past without being confined by museum standards of historical accuracy. One exchange between the First Lady and du Pont concerning a piece of furniture highlights their different approaches to restoration. The object in question was an imported Federal-period mirror that featured an eagle in its design. Ambivalent over whether or not this item of French manufacture should be displayed in the White House, du Pont inquired if Mrs. Kennedy felt it should be accepted. She replied, "I think the mirror should be accepted if you like it. As long as it has the eagle, it doesn't matter if it's French."[22] This statement illustrates not only Jacqueline Kennedy's priorities in selecting period furnishings but her keen awareness that the project was being exposed to public scrutiny, and that the public might fault her for accepting a French mirror, or at least a French mirror that wasn't decorated to attract the fancy of the early American consumer.

Obviously Henry du Pont could not monitor the daily activities of the White House Curator's office. His trips to Washington were irregular, although he sometimes sent John Sweeney or another colleague to survey the progress of the restoration and report back to him. During his personal visits he was able to grant approval to items that had been sent to the White House for inspection. A typical visit by du Pont to the White House was described by William Elder in a memorandum to Mrs. Kennedy on July 20, 1962:

> Mr. du Pont came in and spent the day here Wednesday and made his usual tour of the House. The chandelier for the library was brought down from New York that day. . . . Mr. du Pont agreed with me that it did not seem to be a period chandelier, and suggested that we have an expert look at it. . . . Janet [Felton] and I went to Philadelphia a few weeks ago and bought some needed furniture for the third floor bedroom, consisting mainly of four bureaus and some mirrors. Mr. du Pont saw them on his visit and approved all of them.[23]

During these visits du Pont was apt to move furniture around as he saw fit. Elder, again reporting to Mrs. Kennedy, described another visit on November 29, 1962, saying:

> Mr. du Pont came by for about an hour this morning and did a little furniture moving. He still wants to remove the comfortable sofa from the Queen's Room and replace it with an early nineteenth century one that we have not yet used anywhere. He also tried the small Duncan Phyfe sofa that was recently put in the Queen's Room in the Library in place of one of the armchairs by the fireplace, and wanted to put it there when the other sofa is put in the Queen's Room.[24]

Elder recalls that after such visits Mrs. Kennedy would have him go through the house replacing items of furniture in the positions they occupied before du Pont's arrival.[25] This example indicates that Jacqueline Kennedy was willing to let du Pont feel that he was responsible for arranging the White House furnishings, when ultimately she retained control of the final decisions.

Being the first Curator of the White House put Lorraine Waxman Pearce in a high-profile position. Her glamorous job, working in the most famous "house" museum in the country, and her access to the Kennedys, made her a highly desirable speaker at society luncheons as well as academic seminars. Being a young, educated wife and mother in a time when working women were still uncommon added to her appeal. The press treated her practically as a novelty. Following the practice of museum professionals, Pearce accepted many speaking engagements, spreading the word about Mrs. Kennedy's project and the long-hidden treasures of the White House to a wide audience. She also authored several articles on the historical furnishings in the White House for *The Magazine Antiques.* The public promotion of the restoration, beyond the scholarly articles, was in direct opposition to Jacqueline Kennedy's fierce desire that the details of the project remain private. Discretion was the mantra of the restoration, applied to everyone from members of the Fine Arts Committee to upholstery vendors. Mrs. Kennedy perceived Lorraine Waxman Pearce as a publicity seeker, a role that prevented her from devoting full attention to the work that needed to be done in the White House. Indeed, the rapid rate at which Mrs. Kennedy and the committee were acquiring furnishings and redesigning rooms created a heavy volume of work in the Curator's office, especially when the Curator was trying to maintain museum standards for accessioning and cataloguing the newly designated "permanent" collection.

Not the least of Pearce's burdens was having to serve too many masters. She was at the center of a project being run by a committee, a more-or-less independent chairman, a foreign decorator, and a formidable First Lady. Pearce recalls her frustration in attempting to administer the Curator's office professionally, remembering that there was very little structure and a lack of organization as to procedures for dealing with the work.[26] Naturally this situation led to a great deal of frustration on her part, and she confided this to her mentor du Pont in her frequent letters to him at Winterthur.

Some members of the Fine Arts Committee were aware of the difficult position in which Pearce found herself. A letter from Marvin Schwartz, a member of the Advisory Committee, to du Pont in June 1961, after a visit to the White House, reveals not only his concern for Pearce but also the ineffectual nature of the Advisory Committee. Referrring to himself and James Biddle (another Advisory Committee member, who accompanied Schwartz on this visit), he stated:

> Lorraine's job, we both felt, is a most difficult one and we wished we could be of greater assistance. I wondered if some kind of system could be worked out whereby some of us as near as New York could help and actually sweat a little on the project. I wouldn't think it beneath me to fly down to Washington once a month to catalog or do any other routine matter that would help speed up the project.[27]

James Biddle, in response to the same visit, wrote du Pont with concern regarding his authority in approving all items considered for acquisition by the White House, saying, "Everything that comes to my attention I forward on to you for your decision. Such, I gather, is not always the case. . . . Lorraine feels and we [Biddle and Schwartz] agree that she must approach her work from the curatorial point of view and not merely serve as a coordinator of a variety of decorating whims."[28] Biddle's suspicion that not all objects coming into the White House were approved by du Pont was accurate. The public image of the restoration as a professional project under the control of a committee was a façade. Gradually, Mrs. Kennedy and a few members of the committee took more liberty in determining which objects were accepted and where they were displayed. It was an atmosphere in which the Curator had minimal control.

Ultimately, Lorraine Waxman Pearce took a sabbatical from her duties. She was given an office in the Department on the Interior in order that she could concentrate solely on completing the text for the White House guidebook being produced in conjunction with the White House Historical Association. This Association was established in 1961 for the publication of the guidebook and to sponsor public programs involving the White House. After the guidebook was published in August 1962, Pearce officially resigned her position. Soon after, William Voss Elder III was appointed Curator and James Ketchum, an employee of the National Park Service, was brought on as registrar. In writing to du Pont immediately after her resignation, Pearce expressed her relief at being free from the pressures of the White House and the near futility of trying to uphold the high standards set for the project in such a confusing atmosphere.[29]

Despite the sometimes difficult circumstances, du Pont and Elder persevered in their mission. After their initial meeting in February 1961, the Fine Arts Committee did not meet regularly. Communication between members was sporadic, occurring when certain advice was needed regarding an acquisition. By late 1962 the committee was generally regarded as inactive by inside participants in the project. William Elder recalled that when an object came up for consideration, he and Janet Felton facetiously referred to themselves as "the Committee" and they alone would vote to accept or decline an item.[30] The only members to attend the infrequent meetings were close friends of Mrs. Kennedy's. However, du Pont continued to make occasional visits to the White House and also advised Elder and other participants on furnishings and room arrangements.

William Elder, having worked with Lorraine Waxman Pearce since the beginning of the project, was well aware of the constraints placed upon the Curator. He too strove to maintain museum standards in creating historically accurate period rooms in the White House. However, unlike his predecessor, he did not seek publicity from his position and worked efficiently among the decorators, historians, and socialites who populated the project at various times during his tenure in the White House. This fact did not go unnoticed by Jacqueline Kennedy, who greatly valued Elder's loyalty and discretion.[31]

Elder did, however, feel frustrated at trying to maintain museum standards in the face of the sometimes contradictory efforts of Jacqueline Kennedy and Stéphane Boudin. Writing to du Pont in January 1963, he expressed his alarm: "Mr. Boudin was here for two days last week, and I have wanted to write to you ever since his visit. I feel that a lot of damage will be done to the White House unless you or someone else on the Committee speaks to Mrs. Kennedy. The Blue Room has been completed and whether it is authentic or successful cannot be remedied at the present time."[32] The highly controversial redecoration of the Blue Room, which will be fully described in a later chapter, was the work of Boudin. Of all the State Rooms, the Blue Room, with its lush wall coverings and upholstery, represented the extent to which Boudin had infiltrated the White House restoration.

Elder worried about other rooms that had fallen under Boudin's influence. His conflicts with the influential decorator caused him to question the purpose to the Fine Arts Committee. He wrote to du Pont: "I have tried to warn Mrs. Kennedy with little success and sometimes I wonder why I am even working here. However, I do feel the time has come to decide whether the Fine Arts Committee has any say in the White House or whether it should even exist. Mr. Boudin may be all right as a decorator but he has absolutely no knowledge or respect for American furniture or paintings."[33] In response to Elder's disheartening report, du Pont acknowledged the difficulty of the situation. While recognizing that "conditions are infuriating," he urged Elder not to be discouraged.[34] Elder left the White House in the fall of 1963 to take a position with The Baltimore Museum of Art; he was succeeded by James Ketchum, who remained in the Curator's position until 1970.

Despite the usual portrayal of Henry du Pont as the duped decorator, he did not publicly convey any sense of being personally or professionally betrayed by Jacqueline Kennedy's affinity for Stéphane Boudin. John Sweeney recalls that du Pont was aware that his recommendations were not always followed and that he was not surprised that his room arrangements were altered. He viewed the decoration of the White House as the prerogative of Mrs. Kennedy and was honored to be asked by her to assist with the restoration. It was not unusual for du Pont to be flattered by friends and colleagues who invited him to their homes to offer his esteemed advice on arranging furniture. He knew that, in many cases, the furniture was returned to its original location after he left.[35] Ironically, du Pont commented on this phenomenon in an interview with Harlan Phillips in April 1962, during the height of his

The second Curator of the White House, William Voss Elder III, shown holding the Grandma Moses work entitled The Fourth of July. *This painting was temporarily removed from Caroline Kennedy's bedroom for inclusion in a 1962 exhibition on the noted twentieth-century artist. Private Collection.*

involvement in the Kennedy White House. Without directly referring to Mrs. Kennedy, he may have been alluding to his knowledge of Boudin's influence in her project. In fact, the professional staff of the Curator's office were more discouraged by having to work with Boudin and his decorators than was du Pont.

In spite of all of the behind-the-scenes negotiations between decorators and dealers, politicians and socialites, the Kennedy White House "restoration" progressed with greater success than any previous similar attempts, both in terms of its physical results and public approval. The public's view of the project can be attributed to the massive amount of attention paid to the White House in the media, which, in general, praised Mrs. Kennedy's efforts

James Roe Ketchum, a National Park Service employee, was brought into the White House to assist in the busy Curator's Office. In October 1963, at the age of twenty-four, he was asked to take over as Curator upon the departure of William Elder. In this photograph he is shown in the restored White House Library handling a Willard clock presented by the Americana Foundation. Courtesy John F. Kennedy Library.

as the metamorphosis of the White House from a residence to a national shrine was chronicled across the country.

Certainly the most enduring media image of the restoration is of Jacqueline Kennedy welcoming the nation into her home during the televised tour that originally aired on February 14, 1962. According to CBS network officials, "it was the greatest sight-seeing trip in history."[36] Over eighty million viewers watched the event; the overwhelming tide of positive response for the television program was unprecedented. The refurbished White House became part of the cultural renaissance that the Kennedys were credited with bringing to Washington and the country as a whole. Following Mrs. Kennedy through the rooms of the White House, listening to her breathless descriptions of the rediscovered historical furniture and paintings, few viewers could imagine the enormous amount of detail and intrigue taking place behind the scenes. Maxine Cheshire aptly described the story of the restoration for

Newsweek in 1962, calling it "a tale that encompasses scholarship, wrangling over prices, discreet pressure, petty jealousies, and a cast of influential characters who keep well behind the velvet curtain Jackie has drawn around the inner workings of her program."[37] Now, that velvet curtain is lifted to reveal more clearly than ever before the roles these individual characters played and the result of their collective efforts.

CHAPTER THREE

Maison Blanche

"Jackie Kennedy," wrote Diana Vreeland, "put a little style into the White House . . . and *suddenly* 'good taste' became good taste."[1] This statement suggests that John and Jacqueline Kennedy moved to 1600 Pennsylvania Avenue with an unparalleled sense of style. However, although both had a sensitivity to history and culture through their privileged backgrounds, they had not yet formulated the sophisticated elegance that we associate with the Camelot legacy. What the Kennedys lacked in direct knowledge as true connoisseurs on Inauguration Day they more than made up for with access to society's great espousers of taste.

Among the influential players in the shaping of the presidential aesthetic was Frenchman Stéphane Boudin, president of the world-renowned decorating firm Maison/Jansen. Introduced to Francophile Jacqueline Kennedy by Jayne Wrightsman, Boudin became the chief creator of one of the most dramatic backdrops ever made for an American presidency. He formulated the decoration of both public and private rooms, utilizing the acquisitions of the Fine Arts and Paintings committees as well as the often opposing opinions of Henry Francis du Pont and Sister Parish. Boudin, along with his talented staff of designers, artisans, and craftsmen, created much of what Diana Vreeland called "a little style" and what *TIME* magazine deemed "a richer, more tasteful, more authentic look to the interior [of the White House]."[2] In the process, Stéphane Boudin provided Jacqueline Kennedy with a personal introduction to French antiques as well as an enhancement of her own definition of the aesthetic.

LEFT: *Stéphane Boudin photographed by First Lady Jacqueline Kennedy in late 1961. He is shown in the Treaty Room as it was being redecorated under his direction. Courtesy John F. Kennedy Library.*

Jayne Wrightsman today. Mrs. Wrightsman introduced Stéphane Boudin to Jacqueline Kennedy and acted as liaison between Jansen and the White House throughout the restoration. She and her husband, Charles, arranged for the initial meeting between Mrs. Kennedy and Henry du Pont. Courtesy Jayne Wrightsman.

Stéphane Boudin was born October 28, 1888, in Paris. His father, Alexandre, designed and made passementeries. Stéphane attended the College de Juilly and later joined his father in business. While showing the latest trimmings to Henri Jansen, founder of Paris's leading decorating firm, Maison Jansen, Boudin's "talent for design, detail, and proportion"[3] was greatly admired. In 1923, at the age of thirty-five, Boudin joined Jansen.

At that time Jansen was far from the small furniture shop originally established on the Rue Royale in 1880. With the successful restoration of the Belgian royal palace at Lacken and landmark displays at the 1899 Franco-Russian exhibition in Saint Petersburg and the 1900 Paris Universal Exposition, Jansen had evolved into an independent resource for everything needed or desired for the interior. Cabinetmakers, carpenters, carvers, painters, gilders, upholsterers, bronze-workers, and engravers were assembled along with an impressive reference collection of pattern books, period textiles, and period furnishings. By 1923 Jansen was an international house of design focused not just on contemporary fashion but on historical interpretation as well.

Boudin immediately became a valued player in Jansen's continuing development. He personally encouraged and supervised the firm's abilities to replicate historic interiors, perfecting period paint techniques as well as the creation of various patinations and distress finishes. Becoming president of the firm in 1936, Boudin guided Jansen's acquisitions of numerous eighteenth-century paneled rooms for incorporation in projects around the world. They became trademarks of the Jansen interiors of the mid-twentieth century.

As Jansen's premier voice, Boudin led the way in translating the French style of interior design to new and established residences throughout the world. He counted among his clients the elite of many worlds, including the Duke and Duchess of Windsor, the Shah and Empress of Iran, Lady Mendl (Elsie de Wolfe), the William Paleys, the Winston Guests, and the Charles Wrightsmans. From the mid-1930s to the time that he worked at the White House, Boudin aided Lady Olive Baillie with the restoration and redecoration of Leeds Castle, Maidstone, Kent, England. Historian John Cornforth noted in a 1983 essay that the Frenchman's English commissions immediately influenced a more subdued national taste: "Not only have fittings that he [Boudin] supplied from Jansen been copied here so that their origin is now forgotten,

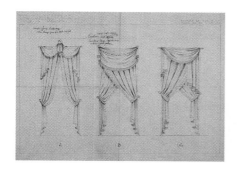

ABOVE: *Drapery designs produced by Jansen for unknown White House interior, possibly the First Lady's bedroom, ca. late 1963. Courtesy Paul Manno. Photo: Jim Frank.*

RIGHT: *Maquette made by Jansen of New York; dining room of Mrs. Robert Allen, New York. This is similar to the maquette made of the Blue Room of the White House and illustrates the level of detail in proposals created by both the Paris and New York offices of the prestigeous firm. Courtesy Paul Manno. Photo: Jim Frank.*

but . . . virtually all specialist painters employed by English decorators have absorbed at least some aspects of Boudin's teachings."[4]

Boudin's influence on American interiors was equally subtle. For Charles and Jayne Wrightsman, collectors of French decorative arts, Boudin provided a crucial introduction to eighteenth-century interior design. Boudin, assessed one-time National Gallery of Art Director John Walker, "was a magnificent teacher, and Jayne a devoted pupil."[5] Together they transformed a Georgian-style Palm Beach mansion into a French château of the sort overlooking the Riviera. Boudin also designed the couple's Fifth Avenue apartment as well as formulated the general concept of the Wrightsman galleries and period rooms at the Metropolitan Museum of Art in New York.

Through his years as Jayne Wrightsman's tutor and decorator, Boudin was subsequently introduced to a number of her friends, among them Jacqueline Kennedy. The Kennedy-Wrightsman friendship no doubt began with both women admiring the station held by the other; where Kennedy was enamored of Jayne's knowledge, taste, and material wealth, the insightful Wrightsman may have been equally intrigued with the future prospects of her younger friend. Wrightsman wrote a letter of introduction to Boudin for Jacqueline Kennedy, and soon "she too fell under his spell."[6] At the time, the wife of the then-junior senator from Massachusetts was adhering to a tight budget set forth by her husband. "New York [antiques] dealers," remembers one acquaintance, "would basically refuse to deal with her because whatever

Paul Manno, Director of Jansen's New York office, ca. 1960. Courtesy Paul Manno.

they sent for consideration was inevitably returned . . . she didn't have the money to spend that her friends had."[7] Written approximately five years before John F. Kennedy was elected President, the Wrightsman letter noted in its concluding paragraph, "Who knows—she may some day be First Lady."[8]

Once this prophecy was transformed into reality, Jayne Wrightsman became uniquely involved with the restoration of the White House. In addition to arranging the introductory lunch between Jacqueline Kennedy and Henry du Pont, connoisseur of American decorative arts and then-hopeful chairman of the White House Fine Arts Committee, she and her husband, Charles, financed many aspects of the restoration project. Jayne Wrightsman was an invaluable participant who was very good at delegating responsibilities as well as at making sure to "suggest having it done . . . at Jansen where it would be beautifully done."[9] (Her dedication to the restoration project was evidently not dependent on the fact that her good friend was the incumbent First Lady. Regarding the redecoration of the Yellow Oval Room, Jayne Wrightsman noted that she wanted to make sure that the likely next First Lady—as far as she was concerned—approved of the decorations as well: "The more I think about it the more I think that gilt furniture with the plain painted walls might be too pompous—particularly for Mrs. Nixon!")[10]

"Having it done" by Jansen was accomplished using a variety of channels of communication. This was necessary because Boudin's schedule limited his actual visits to the White House to less than a dozen during the two-year, ten-month tenure of the Kennedys (one of these was to attend a State dinner for the French Minister of Culture, André Malraux). This fact reveals that many of the interior schemes were formulated by Boudin through telephone and mail correspondence with others. Paul Manno, Director of Jansen's New York office, was the main translator of Boudin's ideas for the White House. Indeed, the majority of the renderings and measured drawings for the project were produced in the New York office under Manno's meticulous supervision, which should have relieved the White House of any criticism about work being done by foreigners. (However, a number of the most important proposals, including the original concept for the Red Room and proposals for the Blue Room upholstery, were prepared in Paris under Boudin's direct supervi-

Arthur Kouwenhoven, a designer in Jansen's New York office, did much of the field work for the White House project. Private Collection.

sion. It appears that even some draperies, like those ordered for the Green Room and the President's Oval Office, were fabricated in France as opposed to the United States.)

Paul Manno remembers that Boudin never visited the White House "without me," and this reveals a special bond between the elder Frenchman and the chief of Jansen's New York office. Indeed, from the time that he started as an office boy in 1937 to his succession to the New York directorship twenty-two years later, Manno evolved from an eager apprentice to the loyal confidant of the "master." With regard to the White House project, it was Manno who kept track of the ever-changing White House wish list, and it was he who immediately knew what Boudin envisioned for the painting of a specific interior—like the paneling of the mansion's Vermeil Room—when the memory of another commission from twenty or thirty years before was cited. Manno also met with Boudin abroad: "I am leaving for Paris on Monday 24tg [*sic*]," noted Manno in a letter to the White House, "and I wish to discuss with Mr. Boudin the type of curtains for the Gold and China Rooms, and I will send you the drawing from Paris."[11] This partnership of talent and organization was crucial to the success of many Jansen projects, particularly the restoration of the White House.

The New York office at 1 East 57th Street had a staff of six that included Paul Manno and two additional designers, Harold Eberhard and Arthur Kouwenhoven, as well as two draftsmen, Leo Monti and Roger Bengue. Manno appointed Kouwenhoven the field person for much of the White House–related work, which entailed finding samples of specific textiles and fulfilling requests for lamps, tables, and other items; he also traveled to Washington to supervise installations of draperies and wall treatments. Leo Monti fabricated the precise miniature rooms, or maquettes, that allowed the decorators to successfully convey proposals to clients like C. Z. Guest and Babe Paley as well as First Lady Jacqueline Kennedy. Monti and Bengue's renderings for dressing tables, seating furniture, stair railings, etc., were works of art in themselves. Without question, the talent within Jansen's New York office, like that offered by the firm's Paris headquarters, had few, if any, true rivals. "Jansen is the one to do it with," wrote Jacqueline Kennedy to her successor, Lady Bird Johnson, "as they are in everything. . . . Everyone else is too decoratorish—they are the only firm . . . with a library of historical documents & artisans to execute them."[12]

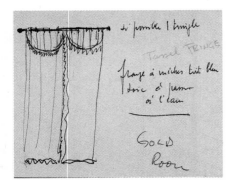

Stéphane Boudin's sketch for the window treatment in the Vermeil Room of the White House. Using sketches such as this, the artists at Jansen formulated working drawings for formal proposals. Courtesy Paul Manno. Photo: Jim Frank.

While depending on Jansen's New York office to supervise the Presidential commission, Boudin maintained direct communication with the White House. From Paris, the president of Jansen wrote "hundreds" of letters to J. B. West, the mansion's Chief Usher, who was responsible for scheduling and supervising the many changes. Boudin forwarded everything from drawings to paint colors to West: "Kindley [*sic*] will you find herewith two different samples of colour for the Room 303 [a third-floor guest room] to go with the chintz you have sent a sample to me lately."[13] West was also responsible for making sure that bills were paid, a most difficult task when one recognizes that some projects involved directing payments to both the Paris and New York offices of Jansen. (One incident of misdirected money took the Paris and New York offices two years to clear up with the White House.) West's exchanges with Boudin led the First Lady to jokingly surmise that "you are carrying on one of the great French correspondences of the century. . . . I think you two are having a great affair!"[14]

As he had for Jayne Wrightsman, the Frenchman served as Jacqueline Kennedy's personal tutor, training her eye with regard to color, proportion, and arrangement. His actual visits to the White House were coveted by the First Lady, who made sure to clear her schedule so as to devote all attention to Boudin. But even when not at the White House, the inclusion of "sample from our friend," or the more specific "S. B. to order in Paris," "S. B. to send estimate," and "as described by S. B." in memoranda and letters to and from the White House emphasized his importance as defined by the First Lady. Furthermore, his influence was not limited to the mansion's State floor. By 1963 Boudin began a complete overhaul of Sister Parish's post-Inaugural redecoration of the First Lady's bedroom and the President's Oval Office as well as the development of plans for the bedrooms of the Kennedy children.

Perhaps mirroring the extent of his involvement with the lives of other clients like Jayne Wrightsman, Boudin extended his advice beyond the walls of the President's official residence. "This is a sample of the colour of the Duchess of Windsor's Boudoir," wrote Boudin to West on behalf of the First Lady, "which . . . [I] send to Madame Kennedy for her house in Virginia."[15] Although the First Lady selected another color for the living room of her newly completed weekend house, she accepted Boudin's suggestions for a variety of other aspects of decorating the Kennedys' personal sanctum.

Sheelagh Manno, wife of Jansen's New York Director, with Stéphane Boudin shortly before his death, ca. 1966. Courtesy Paul Manno.

So treasured was Boudin's knowledge that the First Lady personally assembled an album documenting the changing White House rooms for presentation to the Frenchman. Even after leaving the White House and moving to New York, Jacqueline Kennedy acknowledged his importance. When the weak and dying Boudin was in Manhattan for one of the last times, the former First Lady invited him to lunch at her Fifth Avenue apartment. Accompanied by the loyal Paul Manno, Boudin was asked to advise on the placement of furniture and artwork. The request was a tribute to Boudin, for no sooner had he departed than the room was returned to its pre-visit appearance. "It was a very nice gesture on Mrs. Kennedy's part," remembers Manno. "She made Boudin feel appreciated."[16]

To the end of her own life, Jacqueline Kennedy Onassis saw Stéphane Boudin as much more than an interior designer. In 1992 she guided Mark Hampton with his chapter on Boudin for his book *Legendary Decorators of the Twentieth Century,* sharing remembrances of the famous Frenchman. When Hampton wrote that Boudin had been chosen to help with the restoration of the White House "over native-born decorators because his European background had accustomed him to working on a monumental scale in houses of heroic proportions . . ."[17] he was no doubt paraphrasing the book's editor, the former First Lady herself. She was quoted in 1980 as saying: "When you saw him [Boudin] work, you saw what no American decorator could do. . . . [he gave the rooms] a sense of state, arrival, and grandeur."[18] World-renowned Boudin was one of Jacqueline Kennedy's most influential tutors with regard to establishing her own sense of taste. But more important, he was the creator of much of the visual imagery associated with Camelot—a mythical legacy that she helped to establish in the days following her husband's assassination and which she continued to honor to the time of her own death in 1994.

CHAPTER FOUR

The State Dining Room

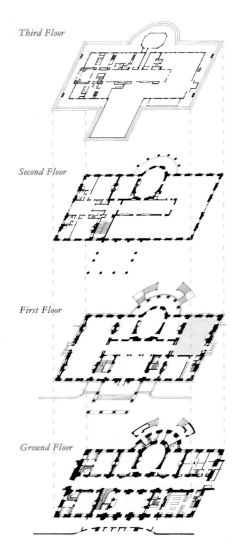

Third Floor

Second Floor

First Floor

Ground Floor

With the Kennedys a new emphasis on entertaining came to the White House, and the State Dining Room was transformed with paint and gilt to reflect its important role as the setting for many elegant evenings. From the simple to the dramatic, a series of changes and additions to the room were initiated by the various players in the restoration. Henry du Pont, Sister Parish, and Stéphane Boudin all participated in a reappraisal of the mansion's main dining room. However, the most influential tastemakers were Beaux Arts-trained architects McKim, Mead, and White, who had reconfigured the room sixty years before for Theodore Roosevelt, the nation's first "modern" president.

Praise of McKim, Mead, and White's work was expressed during Jacqueline Kennedy's February 1962 televised tour of the mansion. "This room's interesting," she explained while walking in the Roosevelt-commissioned State Dining Room, "because it has the most architectural unity of any room in the White House."[1] That the space still spoke so strongly of the motivation behind Theodore Roosevelt's turn-of-the-century renovation—a conscious desire to create a symbolic and historically based backdrop representative of the United States's then new-found strength as a world power—was surely as important to Jacqueline Kennedy's praise as the homogeneity of the room's various elements. Indeed, Roosevelt's efforts to redefine the mansion's role as a national symbol were similar to Mrs. Kennedy's own attempts to bring period antiques and fine art into the rooms. Thus, Roosevelt's backdrop,

PAGE 54: *Completed installation of the mantel in the State Dining Room, 1962. Courtesy John F. Kennedy Library.*

BELOW: *The completed State Dining Room of the White House in October 1962. Courtesy John F. Kennedy Library.*

as created by McKim, Mead, and White, existed as an object of admiration and, more important, emulation.

Both Stéphane Boudin and Fine Arts Committee chairman Henry du Pont made suggestions for enhancement of the State Dining Room's appearance. As expected, Boudin's ideas were based heavily on European—mainly French—design principles, while du Pont's adhered closely to a period room philosophy where furniture, textiles, and architecture were intended to represent a set time frame. Like other White House interiors, the completed decoration of the formal dining room was a combination of the talents and tastes of the two men.

During his first walk-through in February 1961, Boudin made general recommendations for the decoration of each room. For the State Dining Room, he advised painting the existing celadon-colored paneled walls an off-

"Grande Salle à Manger, face de la cheminée."
Design for mantel in the State Dining Room by
Jansen, March 3, 1961. Courtesy Paul Manno.
Photo: Jim Frank.

white. In the process of walking around the large table with its gathering of high-backed, gold silk-upholstered chairs, the Frenchman suggested gilding the existing silver-plated chandelier and sconces. Boudin next recommended replacing the simple, dark marble fireplace surround, installed during the Truman administration's renovation of the mansion, with a more traditional white marble example. In fact, he knew of an ideal mantel design for the room, which included a large eagle in its central tablet. In the weeks after returning to Paris, Boudin forwarded a drawing of the proposed mantelpiece to the White House for consideration.

Henry du Pont seemed to have been in agreement with most of what Boudin suggested. He supported the proposed change in wall color, which Sister Parish arranged to be done by New York's Peter Guertler as a donation to the restoration. Du Pont also apparently agreed with the proposed gilding of the lighting fixtures. Prior to the reinstallation of the chandelier and sconces, he suggested that the wall fixtures be set within panels as opposed to returned to their original locations on the fluted pilasters. He also believed that a new mantel should be found for the room. However, du Pont was not interested in Stéphane Boudin's proposed eagle design. Instead, he supported researching the possibility of the return of the original McKim, Mead, and White mantel, which was by then part of a permanent exhibition at the Harry

Installation of reproduction of the original mantel made by McKim, Mead, and White in the State Dining Room, June 21, 1962. Courtesy John F. Kennedy Library.

S. Truman Presidential Library in Independence, Missouri. By mid 1961 an effort to acquire the original mantel had proved unsuccessful, and a new proposal was made to install a reproduction.

Duplicating the Roosevelt-era mantel satisfied both the du Pont–led interest in preserving the original turn-of-the-century character of the State Dining Room and Boudin's belief that the room should have a basic white and gold color palette. The original McKim, Mead, and White mantelpiece was made of unpolished gray stone, a coloring and texture suitable to the baronial waxed-oak walls of Roosevelt's day but one that would not have been flattering to the regal, off-white painted paneling of the Kennedy redecoration. Thus the reproduction was made of highly polished white marble. It was delivered to the White House in the summer of 1962 and presented as a gift of both the Marble Industry of New York and Steinmann, Cain, and White,

Lorraine Waxman Pearce with workers inspecting the reproduction mantel on June 21, 1962. Courtesy John F. Kennedy Library.

the successor firm of the illustrious McKim, Mead, and White. Alice Roosevelt Longworth, Theodore Roosevelt's oldest child, joined in the dedication ceremony.

To continue the Boudin scheme, alterations were made to other Roosevelt-era elements of the room. The large mahogany and marble serving table with the eagle base and the matching pair of console tables, which Stanford White modeled after an eighteenth-century English example in his own collection, were painted the same ivory as the walls per Boudin's suggestion. Du Pont seems to have supported this transformation, and he expressed interest in its completion. In a November 22, 1961, letter to Boudin's great patron, Jayne Wrightsman, Henry du Pont noted that he "went to see [painter Peter] Guertler, and when he goes to the White House next Monday . . . he is, State dinners permitting, going to gild the eagles and also put some gilt on the

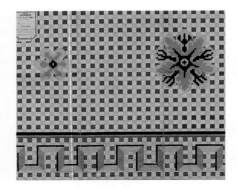

Drawing of the first proposal for carpet in the State Dining Room sent from Jansen's Paris office per the suggestion of Jayne Wrightsman. Courtesy Paul Manno. Photo: Jim Frank.

bowknots or whatever they are and paint the rest of the consoles . . . the same color as the walls."[2] When completed, this change united the tables with the painted paneling of the room while it visually transformed them from eighteenth-century English Georgian to nineteenth-century English Regency.

Presumably du Pont was aware of the origin of this change. However, it is possible that the Frenchman directed his idea to paint the State Dining Room tables through Jayne Wrightsman, who subsequently proposed it, anonymously, to the Fine Arts Committee chairman; this would explain du Pont's detailed update in the letter to Wrightsman. Certainly the transmission of ideas from Boudin through others became necessary as the sensitivity to the foreigner's participation in the project grew. Indeed, both Wrightsman and the First Lady became quite adept at selling the Frenchman's concepts, eventually allowing the "buyers" to see the idea as an extension of their own. This was not limited to the treatment of the State Dining Room tables but included changes throughout the White House.

The painting of the serving and console tables was one of many suggestions for the White House that Boudin adapted from previous commissions. In fact, much of what he planned for the State Dining Room was based on his Anglo-French decoration of Lady Olive Baillie's dining room at Leeds Castle in Kent, England. The painting of the Roosevelt tables made them similar in appearance to a pair of painted, somewhat Adam-style tables he had placed in the Baillie interior. And, although he originally recommended a carpet consisting of gold and black medallions on a gray-blue field, Boudin's final choice of a floor covering for the White House dining room was a reproduction of the Bessarabian carpet purchased for the Leeds Castle dining room.

Presumably Boudin's decoration of Leeds Castle also provided a model for the design of window treatments for the White House State Dining Room. Not installed until 1967, the year of Boudin's death, the straight-falling draperies and stationary, scallop-edged valances were nearly identical in form to examples included in Lady Baillie's dining room. Although records for the design of the draperies do not appear to have survived, the fabric was supplied by Jansen. In recognizing the similarity to Boudin's earlier commission as well as the Frenchman's importance to Jacqueline Kennedy's personal vision for the White House, one may assume that these draperies were in the planning stages at the time of the President's assassination in November 1963.

*Jacqueline Kennedy being escorted through the
State Dining Room following the funeral of
President Kennedy on November 25, 1963. The
Jansen carpet, a reproduction of the one in Leeds
Castle, is shown in the completed room. Courtesy
John F. Kennedy Library.*

All of these changes—proposed and implemented—were seen as extensions of the Kennedys' reappraisal of White House entertaining. Jacqueline Kennedy abandoned the traditional E-shaped banqueting table used by other administrations in favor of a series of individual round tables that sat ten guests each. Made by the White House carpenters, these tables allowed for up to 120 people to be comfortably seated in the State Dining Room, with an additional 30 guests placed in the Blue Room; Mrs. Kennedy served as hostess for the smaller gathering while her husband presided over the dining room. Around the tables the First Lady placed French-style gilt ballroom chairs that nicely complemented Boudin's gold and white scheme. This new format "was a great success," wrote White House housekeeper Anne H.

Lorraine Waxman Pearce with unidentified guests standing before a Chinese coromandel screen first loaned and subsequently given to the White House by Mrs. Boyd Hatch. The screen was originally used in the State Dining Room, where this photograph was taken on July 6, 1961. Later the screen was moved to the mansion's second floor. Courtesy John F. Kennedy Library.

Lincoln, "primarily because it made the protocol-dictated seating arrangements more flexible. Since high-ranking officials were divided among other guests at these tables, the general atmosphere tended to be more relaxed and enjoyable."[3]

For the decoration of tables, Jacqueline Kennedy utilized existing White House possessions as well as new acquisitions. James Monroe's 1817 bronze-doré plateau and baskets, laden with flowers, formed the centerpiece of the President's table, while new vermeil (gilt silver) baskets of similar floral arrangements were used as centerpieces for the smaller round tables. Tulip-shaped crystal glasses purchased from Morgantown Glassware Guild in West Virginia were ordered in early 1961 for use with the existing Truman and Eisenhower china services. Various pieces from the Margaret Thompson

Biddle collection of English and French vermeil, a 1956 bequest to the White House, were used for cigarettes, nuts, and candies. The tables were both elegant and inviting, an assessment that easily could have described the entire State Dining Room.

CHAPTER FIVE

The East Room

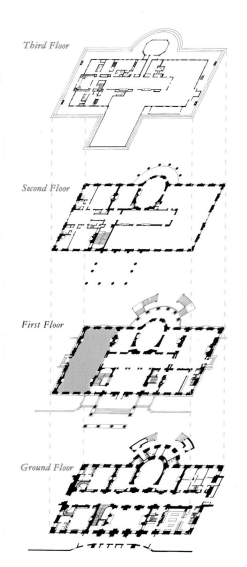

Third Floor

Second Floor

First Floor

Ground Floor

The East Room is one of the more familiar of White House interiors with regard to public identification. Beyond the fact that it is the mansion's largest room, it also has served as the site of many historic events. Daughters of Ulysses Grant, Theodore Roosevelt, and Woodrow Wilson were married in this room, while presidents who have died in office have lain in state under its central chandelier. Familiar stories such as Abigail Adams's drying of laundry in the yet-to-be-completed "great audience" room or Union troops sleeping on its then-carpeted floor have been interwoven in lore through the years. More than any other, the East Room has become the great public room by its simple inclusion in so many aspects of our country's history.

After John and Jacqueline Kennedy moved to the White House, public familiarity with the East Room was enhanced. Although there existed a long tradition of using the East Room for concerts and after-dinner entertainment before the Kennedys, they made the East Room—both literally and figuratively—the nation's premier stage for music, drama, and dance. They invited Shakespearean companies, opera divas, and world-renowned cellists as well as dancers, poets, and actors to perform for kings, princes, and prime ministers. The First Lady even sponsored the creation of a crimson velvet-upholstered portable stage for the room, designed by Lincoln Kirsten. "I just think that everything in the White House should be the best," noted Jacqueline Kennedy during her famous televised tour of the mansion. "[T]he entertainment that's given here . . . if it's an American company that you can help, I like to do that. If it's not, just as long as it's the best."[1]

PAGE 64: *Members of the Shakespeare Festival Theatre of Stratford Connecticut being congratulated by President and Mrs. Kennedy following their performance in the East Room in October 1961. Courtesy John F. Kennedy Library.*

The First Lady devoted seemingly endless attention to both small and large details relating to the East Room's role as an official backdrop for the performing arts. From the appearance of draperies when untied for evening events to the design of attractive portable tables for holding ashtrays and drinks, she attempted to make sure that the decor complemented the performances. "I noticed how awful East Room curtains looked at concert today when drawn," noted Jacqueline Kennedy in one memorandum. "[T]hey are full of wrinkles. . . . I think we should have silk undercurtains—opaque—we could draw for evening—leaving yellow ones looped back. . . ."[2] Eventually these were made from the 730 yards of silk ordered by Jansen for making new undercurtains for all of the State Rooms.

For suitable portable tables, Jacqueline Kennedy consulted various sources. She inquired of the White House's J. B. West:

> Could you call or write Mrs. [Paul] Mellon—and say I asked you to ask her permission—if I could write to the 2 young men who did the Xmas tree. . . . Tell her it is about the pullman car brass and brown glass ash tray stands for East Room. Say I thought as they see so much—in the theatre, props, lights etc. they might know of something inexpensive & good taste—then you could write them—enclose pictures of stand & tell them how many we need & that ash trays must be lifted out. Thanks.[3]

Evidently unsuccessful with this effort, Jacqueline Kennedy asked Jansen to come up with proposals for replacement ashtray stands. The firm's New York office submitted a chic tripod design consisting of "brass bamboo legs and handles and white Carrara glass tops."[4] Jansen subsequently made two of these tables, which were delivered to the White House in January 1963; the cost was $280.00. In February a very pleased Jacqueline Kennedy requested an estimate for fabricating twenty additional tables. Evidently ordering in quantity did not reduce the manufacturing cost; the submitted estimate was deemed prohibitive, and the First Lady subsequently designed replacement stands herself. Based on an existing three-tier plant stand, these less expensive tables were made of dark wood by the White House's talented carpentry shop. Even after finding a more reasonable substitution for the "pullman car" ashtrays, Jacqueline Kennedy commissioned Jansen to make replacement tops of "special gray granite . . . for the pair of [brass bamboo] . . . stands belonging to the White House."[5] For this change Jansen charged an additional $310.00.

President John F. Kennedy during a meeting about the National Cultural Center in the East Room in October 1963. At the left of the photo can be seen one of the portable standing ashtrays designed for the room by Jacqueline Kennedy. Courtesy John F. Kennedy Library.

In seating guests for evening performances, Jacqueline Kennedy utilized existing White House furniture. For herself, the President, and their official guests, she used Mrs. Herbert Hoover's somewhat art-deco gilt upholstered dining chairs, which, by 1961, were being housed in the White House movie theater. Although a large space, the East Room could not accommodate enough of these comfortable chairs for all of an evening's invited guests, especially after the portable stage was set up. Thus, the remaining guests sat on smaller, lattice-backed bentwood chairs, which Jacqueline Kennedy's predecessor, Mamie Eisenhower, had described as what one expected to see at "a

children's party."[6] If proposals were ever made to replace this inherited group of furniture, they were not given as high a priority as other aspects of the East Room's decor.

Of course the additions of ashtrays and temporary arrangements of chairs were less visible than the changes made to the East Room's architecture and daytime presentation, which were mainly dictated by Stéphane Boudin. Presumably, he began his plans for the room upon his first visit to the White House on February 3, 1961. Boudin directed the removal of four Louis XV-style console tables from the piers between the windows; these dated from McKim, Mead, and White's 1902 redecoration. In their place he positioned McKim-designed bronze and crystal torchères previously used in the corners. Finding the brownish-red marble of the room's four mantels and baseboard too strong visually, the Frenchman suggested white replacements; he offered a less expensive alternative of painting the existing stone elements in imitation of white marble in recognition of the significant cost of this proposal. After viewing the completed faux finish, Henry du Pont congratulated the First Lady on such a wonderful idea, probably not knowing where it had actually originated. (Jacqueline Kennedy and Jayne Wrightsman appear to have kept in mind the possibility of replacing the mantels with actual white marble examples. However, this was never seen as priority for the restoration.)

Other changes to the room's decoration came with the progression of research into the mansion's vast history. The removal of two great mid-eighteenth-century English camelback sofas designed by Robert Adam and made by Thomas Chippendale reflected the scholarship that served as the foundation for the Fine Arts Committee's efforts to acquire appropriate antiques for the White House. Although Boudin must have seen the sofas' monumental scale as inappropriate for even the East Room, it was presumably the du Pont—led research into what actually existed in the early-nineteenth-century White House that led to this change. Thus, the inappropriate Truman-era acquisitions were replaced with gilt benches, and the English sofas were quietly returned to their donor.

Through research done by the White House Curator and Jacqueline Kennedy herself, four candelabra used in the East Room during the early nineteenth century were returned to the room. Ordered in 1817 by President James Monroe for the pair of mantels then in the room, these gilt-bronze fix-

tures were attributed to the great French bronze caster Pierre-Philippe Thomire. The First Lady placed them on the two mantels at the southern end of the room, while crystal candelabra of similar period and proportion were used on the north end mantels. (Sometime during the first quarter of the nineteenth century, four of the windows on the room's east wall were covered over to afford the inclusion of decorative niches. Presumably after Monroe's purchase of the candelabra, the niches were replaced by two additional fireplaces, bringing the number for the room up to four.) The candelabra existed as one of the room's few links to the nineteenth century, as the architecture and most of the furnishings reflected the early-twentieth-century changes by McKim, Mead, and White.

Artwork for the East Room consisted of the famous Gilbert Stuart portrait of George Washington rescued by Dolley Madison during the War of 1812, and the later companion portrait of Martha Washington by Eliphalet Andrews. These portraits had been located in the East Room off and on since the 1870s, becoming permanent fixtures during the Hoover administration. To complement them, Jacqueline Kennedy added two loaned canvases representing Washington's favorite nephew, Bushrod, and his wife. Painted by Chester Harding, these portraits were placed in the far panels of the east wall.

From Jayne Wrightsman the White House received a pair of French sconces for inclusion in the East Room. Jansen's New York office recorded in their files that these museum-quality pieces "will be electrified and hung on the panel[s] on either side of the center window."[7] However, handwritten in the margin is the clarification "To be done by Mr. West."[8] This change in who would carry out the proposed project was no doubt one of many made to save money. Although the First Lady relied heavily on Jansen to fabricate or implement the majority of the approved changes for the White House interior, she was not above redirecting projects to those who could accomplish them for less money. The wiring of these sconces, like the manufacturing of the twenty ashtray replacements, was accomplished by salaried White House staff members.

The Kennedy restoration's greatest addition to the East Room was the design of new window treatments. Requiring almost three years of planning and preparation, these draperies were not installed until 1965, over a year after Jacqueline Kennedy moved out of the White House. Part of the delay had to

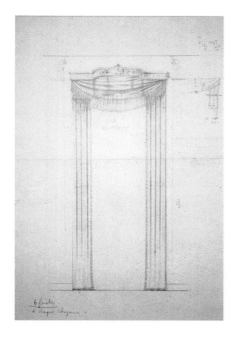

ABOVE: *Design for East Room draperies submitted by Jansen on July 2, 1963. Courtesy Paul Manno. Photo: Jim Frank.*

ABOVE RIGHT: *"La Maison Blanche, East Room." Proposal from Jansen for draperies in East Room, mid-1963. In the process of formulating an accepted plan for the East Room, Stéphane Boudin proposed doing away with valances in all of the windows except the large center window. Courtesy Paul Manno. Photo: Jim Frank.*

do with the formulation of an accepted design. On June 3, 1963, Jansen's Paul Manno forwarded "the document of the fabric which Mr. Boudin proposes for the draperies of the East Room"[9] to the White House. Manno continued his letter by describing the proposed design for the window treatment:

> Only the large center window between the fireplace[s] will have the valance, and the other draperies will be put inside the window boxes.
>
> The draperies will be ornamented with a braid on the edges instead of a fringe and tie-backs will be made in a ball fringe covered with satin of which Mr. Boudin has a lovely antique document.
>
> Please take special good care of this document as this fabric has not been reproduced since 150 years and it is the only sample we have.[10]

It is not clear if Manno's letter was intended to accompany a rendering of the proposed treatment or written as a clarification of a drawing already received by the White House. In a somewhat awkward elevation drawing of this proposal, the elaborate treatment for the central window overpowers the nondescript accompanying design for the remaining six windows. Boudin's intent seems to have been a redirection of focus from the traditional north end of the room, where a large piano was positioned, to the actual center. Certainly Boudin's prior placement of the Wrightsman sconces on either side of the central window suggest an interest in bringing greater attention to the middle of the room.

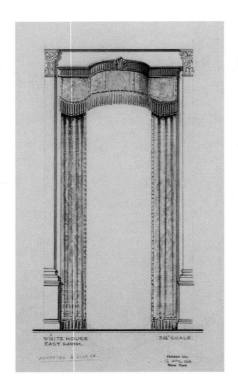

ABOVE: *Rendering of approved East Room draperies from Jansen's New York office, June 3, 1964. Courtesy Paul Manno. Photo: Jim Frank.*

RIGHT: *East Room, ca. 1970, showing Jansen's final drapery design installed. Courtesy White House Historical Association.*

Although the First Lady did not approve this design proposal for the East Room windows—presumably because it did not utilize the existing ca. 1902 gilt wood cornices—she did accept Boudin's submitted textile document. The antique gold and ivory silk lampas had a fifteen-foot repeat consisting of "a fantasy of butterflies, flowers, wheat, a rooster, and numerous cupids busied in various activities."[11] Dating from the early nineteenth century, it was deemed ideal by the First Lady. She approved the document in the summer of 1963 and by fall, even without a formalized design for the window treatment itself, she gave permission for the actual weaving to commence. Thus, all that was needed was an approved drapery design.

In the succeeding months of 1963 Jansen submitted a number of proposals for the East Room windows. All of them incorporated the existing gilt wood valances, per Jacqueline Kennedy's request. At the time of President Kennedy's assassination in November, the final design was still being formulated; not until April 1964 would it be finalized. Although no longer First Lady, Jacqueline Kennedy joined her successor, Lady Bird Johnson, in approving Boudin's proposal of seven sets of straight-falling draperies to be made from "218 meters of [handwoven] cream and yellow lampas, 75 cms wide, specially woven after the antique document shown and retouched as per our drawing."[12] Completing the accepted design were flat valances to be made from "30 meters of brocatelle, little design . . . colors matching the lampas."[13]

Although the brocatelle for the valances was woven and shipped from Paris along with the lampas, it was never used in the actual installation. This elimination was presumably dictated by Boudin from Paris. However, it is possible that the former First Lady was involved in this decision. Mary Van Rensselaer Thayer's book on Jacqueline Kennedy noted that the wood cornices for the windows "had been mostly obscured during the past eight years by the yellow draperies ordered at the time of the Truman Renovation."[14] In that Thayer's biography has been assessed as the closest thing to an autobiography—she interviewed the former First Lady and had access to her private White House files—it is possible that the author was paraphrasing Jacqueline Kennedy's own observation about the importance of the gilt cornices—and, thus, a reason for the elimination of a fabric valance.

The completed treatment consisted of straight-falling panels of the documented lampas trimmed with decorative braid and, at the bottom of each panel, twisted fringe. From the existing wood valances Jansen installed heavy gilt spun-metal fringe. Perhaps in fitting tribute to all that the Kennedy restoration had accomplished for the White House, the more than $26,000 cost of the new draperies was paid for by profits from Jacqueline Kennedy's White House guidebook, which was then in its fourth edition.

CHAPTER SIX

The Red Room

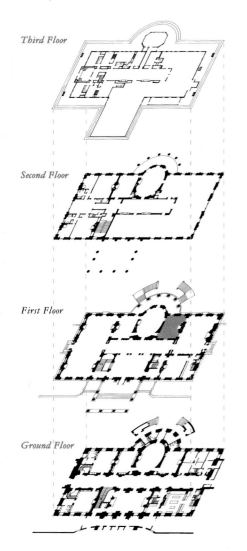

Third Floor

Second Floor

First Floor

Ground Floor

Perhaps there is no better example of the grandeur and drama sought for the Kennedy Presidency than the redecoration of the Red Room. It was the first of the White House's State Rooms to be completely redecorated, and because of its being the first to be redefined with regard to the Kennedy aesthetic, the Red Room served as a testing ground for the diplomacy that was inevitably developed among the numerous "authorities," advisors, and decorators involved with the restoration project. The Red Room also served as one of the few White House rooms for which the First Lady's preference for things French was welcome; it remained her favorite of the State Rooms.

For the Red Room, Emperor Napoleon's France—and its influence on the taste of early-nineteenth-century America that culminated in a style known as American Empire[1]—would eventually set the tone for the furnishings and decoration. In part this was dictated by the architecture of the room, which was a melange of neoclassical motifs, some original to the house's construction, others dating from subsequent renovations. A French Empire mantel with carved caryatid supports, one of a pair originally purchased in 1817 by James Monroe for the State Dining Room and relocated to the Red Room during McKim, Mead, and White's 1902 alterations to the mansion, provided the strongest reason for the adoption of the French Empire taste.[2] The Monroe-era door and window frames and the twentieth-century cornice, chair rail, and wainscoting served as basic complements to the cue set by the mantel.

PAGE 76: *The restored Red Room in early 1962. Shown are Stéphane Boudin's arrangements of portraits on either side of the door leading to Cross Hall. The groupings of three paintings were subsequently replaced with single portaits of Woodrow Wilson and Alexander Hamilton. Courtesy John F. Kennedy Library.*

RIGHT: *Transitional Red Room, mid-1961, featuring the installation of several new acquisitions from the Fine Arts Committee. Courtesy John F. Kennedy Library.*

Also significant to the selection of the Empire style for the Red Room was Jacqueline Kennedy's well-known preference for things French. Indeed, not only for the family quarters but also for the State Rooms the First Lady wanted a Franco-American decor. Many times, as in finding a Jefferson-owned Louis XVI suite for the Green Room or commissioning new French-designed fireplace mantels for the East Room, her wishes went unfulfilled. However, with the Red Room's architecture leading the way, the First Lady was able to contemplate a truly French style for this most important space.

Although Mrs. Kennedy was obviously enamored by the idea of an Empire parlor, it was not the only proposal put forth. Early on, Henry du Pont declared that the room should be decorated with Phyfe furniture. A second proposal came from Fine Arts Committee member Gerald Shea, who attempted to

Early Kennedy-era Red Room showing Jacqueline Kennedy's and Sister Parish's efforts to make this State Room more intimate. The sconces have already been raised to accommodate paintings. The carpet was designed for the White House by Tiffany Studios during the Coolidge administration. Courtesy John F. Kennedy Library.

obtain a suite of American Empire furniture from the Albany Institute, of Albany, New York. In a memorandum to du Pont that underscored the different perceptions of French Empire and American Empire, restoration advisor John Sweeney expressed frustration over the multiple proposals for this room and the lack of organization within the committee. "The situation in the Red Room underlines the problem here, for we have had three different proposals: Empire, Phyfe, and now, Lannuier and French." He went on to characterize the disparate efforts of the committee, identifying "several circles operating . . . [at once] . . . Mrs. Wrightsman leads one . . . [while] Mrs. Parish operates in another and has liaison with people in the trade; Mr. Shea operates in another direction, presumably with the endorsement of Mrs. Kennedy; [and] Mrs. Kennedy herself seems to read Parke-Bernet catalogues and requests that pur-

With our appreciation and best wishes for a happy Christmas
1962

John F. Kennedy   *Jacqueline Kennedy*

The 1962 White House Christmas Card featuring a watercolor rendering of the completed Red Room by artist Edward Lehman. Courtesy Mr. and Mrs. Nash Castro.

chases be made."[3] Sweeney suggested that an executive committee might be set up to coordinate the various groups. However, such a committee was never formed. Although the Albany Institute refused to loan the American Empire suite, du Pont was convinced, no doubt by the First Lady, that Empire— French *and* American—was the best option for the Red Room.

It was not long before individual American and French Empire pieces began arriving for consideration. In time, the centerpiece of the room became

Mr. and Mrs. Henry F. du Pont in the Red Room of the White House in April 1964. Mr. du Pont is standing next to the Lannuier guéridon once offered to him and later acquired by the White House. He considered not buying this table for Winterthur one of his greatest collecting mistakes. Courtesy Winterthur Museum.

a small table (*guéridon*) that had descended in the Livingston family of New York. With caryatids as legs and an intricately designed faux-marble top, this Charles-Honoré Lannuier—labeled piece is still considered the best example of American neoclassical furniture in the mansion.[4] Sofas once belonging to Dolley Madison and Nellie Custis, a sphinx-base sofa table attributed to the French emigré Lannuier, and a pair of elaborately inlaid card tables with sphinx-like supports were also acquired for the room. From White House

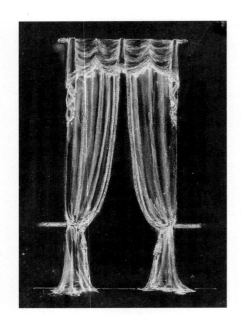

Photostat of Henry du Pont's mid-1961 proposal for new draperies in the Red Room. The valance was to be of solid red material with cotton mull panels. Courtesy Parish-Hadley, New York. Photo: Jim Frank.

storage came four gondola-form side chairs, a pair of transitional American-Empire-to-Rococo-Revival side chairs, and a French Empire armchair with a history of use in the house. Additional pieces were acquired for the room, more than likely under the specific supervision of Jayne Wrightsman and Stéphane Boudin. These included a French gilded wood chandelier, ca. 1820; three French Empire armchairs with gilt-bronze mounts; an enormous French Empire desk; three French bouillotte lamps; a pair of French torchères; and an exceptional Aubusson carpet. (According to Paul Manno, Director of Jansen's New York office, this carpet was greatly admired by Mrs. Kennedy but soon deemed too costly for purchase by the White House. Boudin and Manno approached Wall Street financier André Meyer, whose interest in meeting Mrs. Kennedy provided an incentive for the donation of the French carpet for the Red Room.)[5]

Although socialite-turned-decorator Sister Parish has often been credited with the redecoration of the Red Room, written accounts suggest that she was more a facilitator of sources—donors of furniture and textiles—as well as a kind of switchboard operator who relayed messages between the project players. As both an important member of the newly formed Fine Arts Committee and the decorator of the mansion's family quarters, Parish had an early say in the placement of furniture, and her contributions are evident in photographs showing the Red Room with cozy clusters of chairs and stools and tabletops arranged with framed photographs, flowers, and interesting bric-a-brac. But by mid-1961, when the finer pieces of furniture began to be received and the restoration took on a more scholarly approach with regard to the presentation of the rooms, Parish bowed, graciously or otherwise, to those more familiar with the decoration of such monumental residences. To Henry Francis du Pont, America's authority on period decorative arts, Parish would comfortably pass the reins. However, to Stéphane Boudin, the French interior decorator whose friendship with Jayne Wrightsman had translated into one equally as strong with Jacqueline Kennedy, Sister Parish seems to have given no more than an acknowledgment of his physical existence.

In the first months of the Kennedy Presidency, Wrightsman requested of Boudin period textile documents suitable for reproduction for the Red Room. Although this request was minor in comparison to others soon to be made of Boudin and his staff on behalf of the White House, for Sister Parish

Accepted design for Red Room wall and window treatments, included in a series of proposals sent from Stéphane Boudin to the White House in 1961. Courtesy Parish Hadley, New York. Photo: Jim Frank.

it proved to be a near line in the sand with regard to the continuation of her involvement with the restoration. Already upset about Boudin's suggestions for the Yellow Oval Room on the second floor—an area that had been more or less deemed Parish's personal territory—the New York decorator was angered by the Frenchman's involvement in the decoration of one of the mansion's premier rooms. Presumably Parish felt as though she were being pushed out of what was no less than her most prestigious commission to date. Justified or not in seeing Boudin as a threat, Parish contemplated quitting. "You must *never* think of resigning from the committee," stressed Jayne Wrightsman in a June 28, 1961, ten-page handwritten letter sent from the Hotel Ritz in Paris. "The only thing [Boudin] is doing," continued Wrightsman, "is that . . . I asked him to find an early 19th century document of red color—the *original* color—that could be easily copied in America to re-do the red room [*sic*]. He found a simply lovely document that he would gladly lend to whoever is to make the material [and] he made a design as to how he would put it on the wall."[6] Wrightsman's letter soothed Parish's concerns for the moment, and Boudin's documents were received.

The documents referred to were a series of antique textiles of cerise and gold coloring, which according to Boudin dated from "around 1812."[7] No doubt to Parish's consternation, Boudin also forwarded color renderings for two proposals on how the reproductions of the antique textiles could be used in the Red Room. The first of these schemes included solid cerise silk-upholstered walls framed by a large decorative tape above the chair rail, below the ceiling cornice, and along the sides. This proposal, the Frenchman's favorite of the two submitted, duplicated treatments used in Napoleonic interiors. The second scheme, somewhat more conservative, followed the lead of the first, but eliminated the inclusion of the decorative tape on the sides. This second scheme was, instantly or inevitably, adopted for the Red Room.

If Parish was hoping that Boudin's suggestions for the Red Room would be dismissed by others, she must have been disappointed when in early August 1961 du Pont himself stated that if the manufacturer of the reproduction textiles could get the color right, "I see no reason why we should not order the material now."[8] To Parish fell the responsibility of finding a manufacturer for the reproduction of the cerise and gold decorative tapes as well as fabrics with a variety of special patterns, including a small repeating medal-

Proposal from Jansen's New York office for temporary window treatment in the Red Room, June 1961. Courtesy Parish-Hadley, New York. Photo: Jim Frank.

lion, a very large elongated sofa medallion, and a set of seat and back medallions for armchairs. At first Parish approached the New York firm of Bergamo for the reproduction of Boudin's samples. During the negotiation process Jacqueline Kennedy instructed Parish to see if Bergamo had similarly patterned textiles already in their production line.[9] Presumably this suggestion was intended to offer an alternative should the costs of precisely reproducing the Frenchman's documents be too great. (Reduced costs would no doubt have made a proposal for donation of the finished textiles more attractive to the manufacturer.) The possibility of using stock patterns for upholstery and wall treatments appears to have met with general approval, including that of Henry du Pont, whose main concern was making sure that at least the color of Boudin's sample be reproduced accurately.[10] However, some difficulty must have arisen with regard to Bergamo's participation, for it was not long before Sister Parish showed Boudin's documents to Franco Scalamandré, founder of the New York textile manufacturing company that still bears his name. Scalamandré accepted the challenge of reproducing Boudin's period documents. At this he succeeded admirably.[11]

As the process of finding a manufacturer for the Red Room textiles progressed, so did the completion of the overall decorating scheme for the room. Boudin's second proposal, which had been forwarded with the period textiles, seems to have been the accepted scheme from the beginning as far as Jacqueline Kennedy and Jayne Wrightsman were concerned. However, it does appear that du Pont was not sold on the complete scheme, having reservations concerning the window treatment. His slight discontentedness with the window proposal is verified by an existing photostat of a drawing he sent to Mrs. Kennedy for consideration. Although less skillful in its overall composition than the renderings provided by Boudin's Paris studio, du Pont's proposal was equally elegant. Instead of Boudin's straight-falling panels of cerise silk for the windows, du Pont suggested white cotton voile or muslin panels drawn back with tassels. A separate valance of the same red fabric as that used on the walls was apparently draped over a gilded rod. The First Lady noted to Sister Parish that she thought the use of cotton a great way to brighten what was the darkest of the State Rooms.[12]

However, Mrs. Kennedy does not seem to have liked du Pont's proposal for the windows enough to have chosen it over Boudin's. In part, this deci-

Red Room, view looking south, May 1962.

Courtesy John F. Kennedy Library.

sion may have been based on practicality. In the same letter to Parish that noted the benefit of du Pont's proposal, the First Lady expressed concern over the maintenance of such light and fragile panels. With limited dollars to finance the restoration project, Jacqueline Kennedy made upkeep a very important concern. She made sure that delicate fringes and tassels were not included in window treatments accessible to souvenir-seeking visitors; most of the drapery treatments approved for public rooms incorporated undetachable flat decorative tapes and galloons.

Equally important to upkeep was making sure that window treatments looked their best at all times. In a 1961 memorandum to the mansion's chief usher, Jacqueline Kennedy expressed concern over how unattractive the

Jacqueline Kennedy and Senator Edward Kennedy greeting foreign dignitaries in the Red Room following the funeral of President Kennedy on November 25, 1963. Courtesy John F. Kennedy Library.

draperies in another public room were when drawn closed. She continued by noting that this "is true of all curtains which are roped back in daytimes."[13] Perhaps this explains why only one of the approved redecoration schemes for the State Rooms included window treatments with tied-back panels. More specific to the Red Room, this may suggest why du Pont's fragile treatment for the windows, which would have required constant primping to maintain the desired appearance, was not more seriously considered.

It is also probable that Jacqueline Kennedy was well ensconced in the role of being the student of the "master," Stéphane Boudin. While du Pont was the connoisseur of American antique furniture, Boudin was his equal with regard to decorating. "I've learned more about architecture from Boudin than from all the books I could have read,"[14] confided the First Lady to a staff member. More than likely, Boudin's proposal for new draperies in the Red Room—straight-falling panels of cerise silk suspended from gilded wood rings and rods—like his proposal for the treatment of the walls and the upholstery of the furniture, obtained Jacqueline Kennedy's immediate approval.

For the hanging of paintings, Boudin established a preference for full wall coverage early on. As he had done in the dining room of Leeds Castle as well as other interiors throughout his career, Boudin utilized the entire wall surface of the Red Room for the display of art. In the first round of hanging pictures in this room, with the Truman-Eisenhower–era wall covering still in place, the Frenchman had paintings placed everywhere, including under sconces.[15] After the covering of the walls with the Scalamandré-produced cerise silk in late 1961, Boudin placed two tiers of paintings on the walls: the first tier was at eye level, while the second tier was above door-frame height. The end effect was that of a gallery of paintings, not unlike what one would expect to see in an English or French country house. This was a concept that Boudin had proposed on his first visit to the White House in early February, soon after the Kennedys had moved in, and it was visually restated in the renderings he forwarded to the First Lady the following June.

The redecoration of the Red Room was well received by the public. Requests for photographs flooded the White House, while historic houses throughout the country sought to duplicate various aspects of the room's decor. Scalamandré, which had originally intended to reserve the reproductions of Boudin's textile documents for the White House, eventually made them available to all through special order. Sister Parish received the credit for the decoration of the room because mention of Stéphane Boudin's role in the redecoration of the Red Room would not have met with the approval of the American public.

With our appreciation and best wishes for a happy Christmas
1963

John F. Kennedy   Jacqueline Kennedy

The Green Room

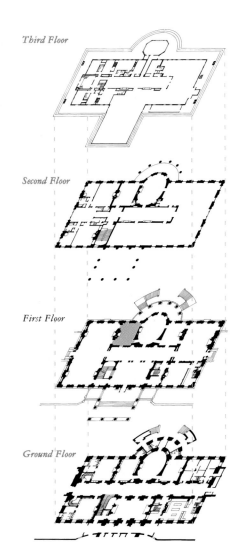

The decoration of the Green Room was accomplished through as near a partnership between Stéphane Boudin and Henry du Pont as was possible. It was the first of the White House State Rooms to be furnished by the Fine Arts Committee. Therefore, Henry Francis du Pont, an authority on American period furniture, founder of the country's premier decorative arts museum, Winterthur, and, most important, committee chairman, was assured the final say with regard to the selection of each piece of Baltimore-, Philadelphia-, and New England–made Sheraton- and Hepplewhite-style furniture. The Frenchman's role was basically that of the organizer and arranger of objects. Although Stéphane Boudin consistently picked at the du Pont–approved furniture—"the proportion is all wrong . . . these should not be so dainty"[1]—he dedicated his talents to bringing the objects and art together. The Green Room became the President's favorite of the State Rooms.

Like the Red Room, its sister parlor, the Green Room had been recreated by McKim, Mead, and White in 1902 to represent a ca. 1820 parlor or drawing room in the French Empire taste. The Beaux-Arts firm had divided the pair of marble mantels purchased by James Monroe for the dining room in 1817, installing one in each of the two parlors. The mantels, along with surviving door moldings from the same period, dictated the remainder of the McKim, Mead, and White scheme. For Stéphane Boudin, a man so focused on proportion and scale, du Pont's selection of late-eighteenth-century-inspired furniture must have seemed a grave mistake. The room, to him, was Empire.

In fairness to du Pont, the Federal style had been selected for the Green Room long before his first walk-through of the mansion in April 1961. Indeed, Federal had been chosen for the room in the 1920s, when Mrs. Calvin Coolidge assembled the country's leading connoisseurs of American antiques to provide direction for the redecoration of the State Rooms. Like the concurrent formation of the American Wing of New York's Metropolitan Museum of Art, the restoration of Colonial Williamsburg, and the creation of *The Magazine Antiques,* Mrs. Coolidge's efforts were in part a reflection of the country's chosen isolationism following the first world war. In justifying this inward focus, the United States experienced a reappraisal of its own history through which the furniture of the founding fathers was deemed appropriate for any and all interiors, whether the architecture warranted it or not. Although few period pieces were assembled for the White House, the purchase of "appropriately styled" reproductions assured the completion of at least the Green Room as a Federal parlor by 1929. With some minor additions, this was the room that the Kennedys inherited in 1961.

Green Room prior to its complete restoration, May 8, 1961. Substitutions of chairs, tables, and paintings are already visible for this tea given by the First Lady. Mrs Kennedy is shown standing between the window and the doorway. Courtesy John F. Kennedy Library.

Knowing nothing of what had taken place prior to his own involvement in the White House, Boudin worked with what du Pont and the Fine Arts Committee added to the already determined scheme. At the same time, the Frenchman attempted to think American Federal. Delicate settees, Martha Washington armchairs—which Boudin detested—urn stands, worktables, and numerous card tables took their places in the room. Although du Pont's inclusion of French bouillotte lamps—candelabras with painted metal shades—may have pleased Boudin, the room was never to be a true success as far as the Frenchman was concerned.

Boudin's presence should not suggest that Henry du Pont cared little about the placement of furniture in the Green Room. After finding the room rearranged upon one of his visits in late 1961, du Pont wrote to Mrs. Kennedy, saying, "I sincerely hope we can see the room together the way I planned it. . . ."[2] He was particularly concerned about the removal of a very delicate Baltimore lady's writing desk and its subsequent replacement with another Baltimore piece, a labeled Joseph Burgess secretary. The exchange had

Green Room of the White House, mid-1961, showing two of the eight Cézanne landscapes owned by the White House following their return from loan to the National Gallery of Art. The paintings were bequeathed to the White House in 1952 by Charles A. Loeser. These two were later placed in the second-floor Yellow Oval Room. The carpet on the floor was designed in 1927 for the Coolidge administration. Courtesy John F. Kennedy Library.

no doubt been made by Boudin, who must have seen the taller, more substantial secretary a better match with the room's eighteen-foot-high ceiling. Du Pont disagreed with the Frenchman's theory: "As I see it, the room is a charming, intimate little room, and everything should be kept in low scale and not have the eye drawn up by the secretary."[3] The lady's writing desk was returned to its du Pont–selected placement, but only for a brief time.

Far more controversial than its temporary removal from the Green Room was the discovery of the provenance of the lady's writing desk. The piece was donated to the White House by Mrs. Maurine Noun of Des Moines, Iowa, in July 1961, amid much excitement. Believed to be one of only four of its kind in existence, the desk was praised by Mrs. Kennedy in her famous February 14, 1962, televised tour of the White House, calling it "our first piece of unsolicited fine furniture." Du Pont himself was so enthusiastic about the acquisition that he recommended its immediate acceptance, "as I feel sure it does not need to be expertized."[4] However, after months of the desk's being on view to the public as the centerpiece of the newly refurbished Green Room, antiques dealer David Stockwell and Curator William Elder unfortunately determined that it was a late-nineteenth-century copy. It was subsequently returned to Iowa and Stéphane Boudin's preferred Burgess secretary was once again placed in the Green Room. (The Burgess desk was replaced in 1963 by a labeled secretary by Annapolis cabinetmaker John Shaw.)

The discovery of the fake desk in the White House was widely publicized, most notably by Maxine Cheshire in her 1962 *Washington Post* series of articles on the restoration, which also brought unsolicited attention to Boudin's participation in the project. Both the President and the First Lady were outraged by the revelation of the desk discovery, particularly so because Mrs. Noun's generosity was made to appear less than genuine. In a letter to Henry du Pont, Jacqueline Kennedy speculated about how details of the project were reaching the media. Emphasizing her policy that no staff speak to the press, she assumed information was being overheard by others and leaked to reporters. The First Lady requested that only dealers whom du Pont completely trusted be allowed inside the White House, stressing that bad publicity would ruin all the good work that the Fine Arts Committee was undertaking.[5] (No doubt Cheshire's exposure of Boudin's role in the restoration was also on Mrs. Kennedy's mind as she penned her words.)

With the assembly of the furniture at its height of public scrutiny, du Pont and Boudin directed their sometimes collective—but more often than not independent—expertise to the selection of textiles for the Green Room. At the beginning the walls and windows retained the Truman-era Robert Adam–inspired silk damask produced by Scalamandré. Du Pont recommended that the existing window treatments be altered; he suggested that instead of outside of the opening, covering the moldings, they be set within the frame to emphasize the architectural surrounds. This must have frustrated Boudin's ever-sensitive eye for proportion even more, for the exposure of the sixteen-foot-high moldings both continued the definition of the room as Empire and exaggerated the "leggy"[6] characteristic of the Federal furniture. This proposal was evidently discussed during a New York meeting between Boudin and du Pont in early 1961. Although Boudin disapproved of the concept, he instructed Jansen's New York office to prepare drawings per du Pont's recommendation. By mid-1961 the temporary window treatments were in place.

Green Room of the White House showing the decor as it was progressing in March 1962. Courtesy John F. Kennedy Library.

For upholstery, Henry du Pont added to the strong contrast of green walls and white architectural detail by selecting predominantly white or cream-colored textiles. A late-eighteenth-century white cotton with delicate green and gold embroidered vines was chosen for a pair of Massachusetts settees, while a Scalamandré-produced ivory silk with a multicolored floral motif was used on a sofa once owned by Daniel Webster. Chairs were covered in either a medallion-patterned white damask, an Adam-inspired green-on-white silk brocade, or a contemporary silk of green, gold, and buff coloring.

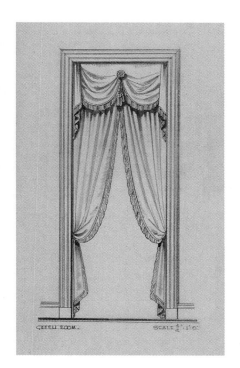

*Jansen proposal for temporary window treatment
in Green Room following Henry du Pont's dictum
that draperies be installed inside the window
molding, June 12, 1961. Courtesy Paul Manno.
Photo: Jim Frank.*

The effect was beautiful, with each piece of furniture reading as a separate work of art against the green of the walls and window treatments.

When the time came to replace the wall coverings and window treatments, Boudin expressed a definite opinion that was, not surprisingly, different from that of du Pont. The founder of Winterthur had submitted to Jacqueline Kennedy his choice of a green stripe—possibly a green-on-green. (This is an interesting selection, for it suggests that much of Boudin's work at the White House was kept secret even from others within the project. It is inconceivable that du Pont would have proposed stripes for the Green Room walls when Boudin had already formulated a plan for stripes to be used in the Blue Room next door.) Boudin supplied his selections, including a late-eighteenth-century moss-colored silk moiré. By mid-1962 the First Lady was obviously leaning more toward the opinions of Boudin and less to the tastes and preferences of du Pont. In one memorandum to the mansion's Chief Usher, J. B. West, she made clear who had the deciding say: "Could you send Mr. du Pont Boudin's 3 samples for green room 1) big ocean on green design 2) smaller green-on-green piece 3) tiny bit of moiré . . . [we'll go ahead with #3]. . . . Please enclose this humble letter soliciting his approval. If we don't get it he will have the shock of me doing it anyway!"[7]

Deeming it a perfect choice for the Green Room in his own mind, or perhaps recognizing that opposition to the selection would not benefit the progress of the project, du Pont endorsed Boudin's sample. The next concern was who would manufacture the reproduction. In a May 29, 1962, letter to Franco Scalamandré, Jayne Wrightsman asked the textile manufacturer to examine the document to see whether or not his firm could reproduce it. Scalamandré quickly responded, noting that the silk had been woven by hand, which explained its great variation in pattern. He also mentioned that only one individual capable of replicating the process was still in business, and whether or not the reproduction textile was acceptable, the man would expect to be paid.[8] Presumably in an attempt to offer an alternative to this risky proposition of handweaving, Scalamandré forwarded to Jansen's New York office a similarly colored sample of silk moiré that had been woven on existing mechanical looms at the firm's Long Island City mill.[9] Although beautiful in its own right, the Scalamandré sample was much thicker and coarser than Boudin's document. Desiring a fabric as close to the original as

Part of an assembled in-house directory of valance treatments used by Jansen's various offices. The top rendering on this page served as the model for the Green Room window valances. Courtesy Paul Manno. Photo: Jim Frank.

possible, Wrightsman replied to Scalamandré that both the First Lady and Henry du Pont believed that proceeding with this project was too great a gamble. She continued by declaring that they "would have to try to find another idea [for the walls] and we will communicate with you later."[10]

In fact, no alternative textile selection was made for the walls of the Green Room. Soon after Jayne Wrightsman notified Franco Scalamandré of the decision not to continue with the moiré project, Boudin took his existing moss-colored document to the Paris-based firm of Tassinari and Châtel, which was celebrating its two hundredth anniversary as one of Europe's leading manufacturers of silks. Tassinari and Châtel maintained the necessary looms and craftsmen to replicate the period moiré document exactly; they provided the variations that had become so important to Jacqueline Kennedy, Boudin, du Pont, and Wrightsman. (At no time during the restoration did the media-sensitive White House acknowledge a foreign manufacturer as the producer of the Green Room moiré. By the 1980s the common belief was that the maker of the Kennedy-era textile was Scalamandré.)

For the windows, Boudin replaced du Pont's temporary insertion of tied-back draperies within the moldings with a standard Jansen design of straight-falling panels covering all architectural details. Instead of installing elaborate swags as valances, Boudin implemented his personal preference for flat panels of fabric ending in a series of Baroque-like tabs or tongues. Both the valances and drapery panels—which a January 1963 Jansen bill for installation records as having "been in Paris"[11]—were made of the same moiré as that used for the walls, trimmed with a French-manufactured decorative tape of silver coloring.

Although variations of the selected valance treatment were included in a number of mid-nineteenth-century English and French pattern books, Boudin's source of inspiration came from a small, hand-assembled pamphlet of line drawings produced by Jansen for exclusive use by its network of offices. Stéphane Boudin simply instructed the artist preparing renderings for the Green Room to use number one from page nine at the windows. (Boudin appears to have favored this particular treatment, for it was incorporated in many of his interiors at Leeds Castle, including the design of the bed canopy in that house's Green Room. He also incorporated a variation of it in the design of a bench for the White House's Queen's Bedroom.)

President and Mrs. Kennedy in the restored Green Room during a reception commemorating the Centennial of the Emancipation Proclamation on February 12, 1963. Courtesy John F. Kennedy Library

With the completion of the walls and windows in January 1963, Stéphane Boudin submitted plans for changes in upholstery fabrics. In February he ordered "35 yards of the striped fabric sample No. Boudin 8856, which will be done in the same color as the moiré."[12] This fabric was intended for all of the side chairs, the Webster sofa, and the pair of settees. For the room's four Martha Washington armchairs, Paul Manno forwarded from Jansen's New York office twenty yards of narrow velvet "the same color as the walls . . . [to] be finished with gilt nails all around the frame and even on top backs as the English chair was done."[13] (It is ironic to note that two of these chairs began their stay in the Green Room upholstered in green velvet, only to be changed to white and green silk by du Pont.) Completing the plan was a green leather, also the color of the walls, that was sent to the White House

The restored Green Room in September 1963. Shown on the table is the curator's guide to the furnishings in the room, left on view for visitors. David Martin's 1767 portrait of Benjamin Franklin, donated by Mr. and Mrs. Walter Annenberg, is above the mantel. On the floor is shown a late 18th-century English Axminster carpet given to the White House by an anonymous donor. Courtesy John F. Kennedy Library.

for use on a recently acquired Louis XVI armchair. By choosing fabrics of the same color as the walls, Boudin hoped to eliminate the visible difference in scale between the room's architecture and the assembled furnishings. Although the reasoning is not clear, only his choice of leather was actually used. The other aspects of Boudin's plans for the Green Room furniture upholstery remained unfulfilled at the close of the Kennedy presidency.

For the arrangement of paintings, Stéphane Boudin concentrated on directing works with elaborate and architectural frames to the walls of the Green Room. There is little doubt that this was another effort to better unite the chairs, tables, and settees with the scale of the room. John F. Kensett's *Niagara Falls* and Theobald Chartran's portrait of Mrs. Theodore Roosevelt took on dual roles. With large planes of gold leaf, applied garlands, and oval openings framing the canvases, these paintings served as both works of art and architectural elements. Small still-lifes were used by Boudin as decorative plaques framing Alvin Fischer's large canvas, *Indian Guides.* The end result was an array of gold forms that neutralized the differing proportions of the fragile-looking furnishings and the room's monumental architecture.

Sensitive to his wife's concentration on French decorative arts in other State Rooms, President Kennedy was politically comfortable in the redecorated Green Room. Without question, it was an impressive representation of an American Federal parlor, and it soon became the President's favorite. The Kennedy family's gift of Claude Monet's *Morning on the Seine,* honoring the assassinated president, was later installed here. It was also in the Green Room that President Richard Nixon placed Aaron Shikler's posthumous official portrait of John F. Kennedy.

CHAPTER EIGHT

The Blue Room

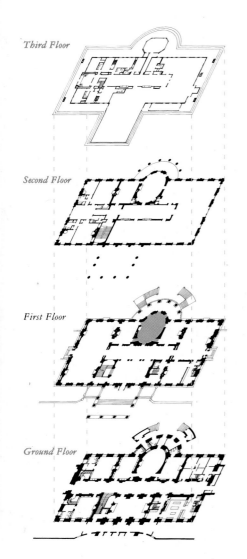

Third Floor

Second Floor

First Floor

Ground Floor

The Blue Room was truly the creation of Stéphane Boudin and the staffs of Jansen's Paris and New York offices. The elliptically shaped room was, from the very early stages of the restoration project, the most controversial of the Kennedy White House interiors. "The Blue Room was Boudin's masterpiece," reflected Jacqueline Kennedy Onassis in 1980. "[It] is a formal reception room, and so you have to have a sense of state, ceremony, arrival, and grandeur. . . . [He] gave it that, and he did it all so simply."[1] Critics of Boudin's Blue Room were subdued when the completed room was opened to the public in January 1963, yet much more vocal after Boudin's scheme was replaced ten years later. In 1985, then–White House Curator Clement Conger described Boudin as "the rage of Paris . . . but he certainly knew nothing about American period houses."[2] Whatever one's opinion, no other White House room better represented the ambitions of the President and First Lady; the Blue Room served as the definitive backdrop for the Kennedy Presidency.

Stéphane Boudin was at home with the Blue Room more so than with any other room in the White House. In part, this feeling of security was instilled by the fact that Charles and Jayne Wrightsman, his clients for more than ten years, were funding its redecoration. This gave Boudin a near-complete freedom that he did not have elsewhere in the project.

Equally important to Boudin's being comfortable with the Blue Room was the history of the room's furnishings. While preparing for her move to the White House in early January 1961, Jacqueline Kennedy began researching the history of the President's house. She read in a 1946 issue of *Gazette des Beaux Arts* about a suite of French gilt furniture originally made in 1817 for President James Monroe's Oval Room by Parisian cabinetmaker Pierre-Antoine Bellangé. A pier table from this suite was illustrated, and Jacqueline Kennedy requested that the White House staff see if it still existed in the house. Chief Usher James West reported that the table did, indeed, exist—however, in less than stable condition. Presumably at either Boudin's or Jayne Wrightsman's suggestion, the White House contacted Paul Manno, Director of Jansen's New York office, to ask if the firm could arrange for the table's restoration. They did just that, and to Jacqueline Kennedy's great pleasure, the table was returned with a new white marble top and gilt finish. The First Lady quickly extended her thanks to Manno, in the process subtly proposing that Jansen consider presenting the completed work as a gift to the restoration. Charmed by Mrs. Kennedy's enthusiasm, Paul Manno agreed to Jansen's underwriting the table's rehabilitation.[3] In appreciation, Jacqueline Kennedy sent Manno an autographed photograph of herself standing before the table accompanied

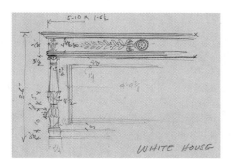

ABOVE: *Jansen's sketch of the Bellangé gilt pier table rediscovered by Mrs. Kennedy, 1961. Courtesy Paul Manno. Photo: Jim Frank.*

RIGHT: *Monroe-era pier table by Pierre-Antoine Bellangé as it appeared upon its "rediscovery" by Jacqueline Kennedy in the basement of the White House, April 1961. Courtesy John F. Kennedy Library.*

by a note that expressed the hope that publicity about the gift might inspire others to be as patriotic as Jansen.[4]

The restored Monroe table, French Empire in style, set the tone for the restoration of the Blue Room. For a while it was used with an existing suite of white and gold chairs—reproductions of pieces made for Napoleon by Jacob-Desmalter—which was fabricated for Theodore Roosevelt by McKim, Mead, and White in 1902. However, Henry du Pont was less than enamored with the Roosevelt suite. It was his belief that if original chairs from the Monroe set could not be found, the Fine Arts Committee should try to find other gilt French Empire examples similar in style to the restored table. This was not to be necessary, for no sooner had the Monroe pier table's restoration been publicized than a Miss Catherine Bohlen of Villanova, Pennsylvania, donated an armchair from the same suite. At the same time, another of the armchairs was noted as being on display in the Tennessee Room of the Museum of the Daughters of the American Revolution in Washington, D.C. Du Pont wrote to Mrs. Kennedy about this chair, saying he was "counting on her to lure this away."[5] Du Pont himself wrote to the honorary President of the D.A.R., Gertrude Carroway, asking for the loan of the chair, as it "seem[ed] cruel that all the [Bellangé] furniture should not be together again."[6] However, the formidable women of the D.A.R. could not be per-

suaded by du Pont's "humanitarian" pleas on behalf of the suite of furniture. The chair was not loaned and the decision was made to reproduce the original armchair—as well as original side chairs located at the Adams National Historic Site in Quincy, Massachusetts—for the Blue Room. Fine Arts Committee member Charles Francis Adams, descendant of both presidents Adams, underwrote seven reproduction armchairs and six side chairs.

With furniture traditionally placed along the walls, Boudin recommended the inclusion of a round table in the center of the room. Presumably it was du Pont who directed the use of a white marble-topped mahogany center table that Monroe had also purchased from France and that had remained in the mansion undisturbed all this time. Although a wonderful table, Boudin must have seen its mahogany columns and base visually in conflict with the Roosevelt-era white and gold chairs and the recently restored gilt pier table. He suggested that the center table be covered with a cloth. Sister Parish selected a gold silk damask trimmed in tassels of the same color. Although Parish's selection was less than to the Frenchman's liking—he believed that it made the piece look "like a fat Spanish dancer"[7]—it did help to better balance visually the center of the room with its perimeter. However, Boudin's covering of one of the oldest possessions to survive in the mansion brought criticism from participants who were already resentful of the increasing role that the Frenchman was taking in the restoration project. It was not long before the substitution of a contemporary table—with a larger version of the

Blue Room, early 1961, showing the rearrange-
ment of the existing ca. 1902 suite of furniture
and the addition of the large center table.
Courtesy John F. Kennedy Library.

Parish-designed tablecloth—was exchanged for the Monroe-era piece; its arrival paralleled the beginning of rumors that "Mrs. Kennedy's French decorator was draping everything in sight."[8]

Although this attempt to cover up such a significant piece of early White House furniture might suggest that Boudin did not have a great appreciation for the history of the mansion, this was not the case. In fact, for the Blue Room, Boudin and Jansen staff members expressed the greatest interest in documentation with regard to original furnishings and decor. The Frenchman and his staff sought answers to a broad range of questions asked of the White House curators concerning original furniture placement and the type of floor coverings used during the Monroe presidency. "The background of the [Monroe] rug was green," wrote Curator William Elder in reference to a Boudin inquiry, "and it is described as having a beautiful border, and the arms of the United States woven in the center. . . . [The] Bald Eagle [was as] 'large as life,' with a scroll in his beak, inscribed with 'e Pluribus Unum,' and with the accompaniment of arrows in his talons; while the flag of America . . . waved over his head."[9] Elder concluded the full page of carpet documentation

Above: Jansen's file folder showing array of textiles and trimmings used in the redecoration of the Blue Room. Courtesy Paul Manno. Photo: Jim Frank.

Below: "The Oval Blue Room . . . copy of maquette from Paris." Scale drawings used for the construction of the model of the Blue Room showing complete proposal for its redecoration by Jansen, March 15, 1962. Courtesy Paul Manno. Photo: Jim Frank.

with the statement, "This is all the information we can supply to Monsieur Boudin." In another memorandum the curator explained the original placement of the famous Monroe pier table: "According to the inventory of 1825 the pier table could only have been opposite the fireplace when you consider all of the other furniture that was in the room."[10] This inquiry referred to the possible inclusion of one of the original nine-foot-long sofas from the Monroe suite that had recently been offered to the White House. (Unfortunately, the addition of two more doorways to the Blue Room at the turn of the nineteenth century made this impossible.)

Boudin's obsession with scale and proportion led to an elaborate process of selecting the correct colors, fabrics, and arrangement of furniture for the Blue Room. Unlike what had been done for other White House interiors, where Jansen's New York and Paris designers concentrated on renderings and textile/color boards to convey proposals, the redecoration of the Blue Room was formulated using a miniature model of the room, known as a maquette. For this oval room twin, artisans made miniature versions of each piece of furniture and every painting to be considered for placement. Drapery treatments for the windows were also prepared to allow Jacqueline Kennedy, Jayne

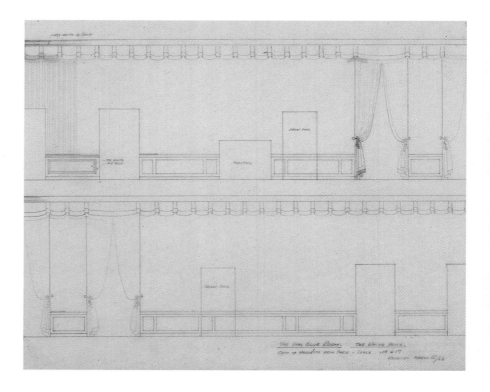

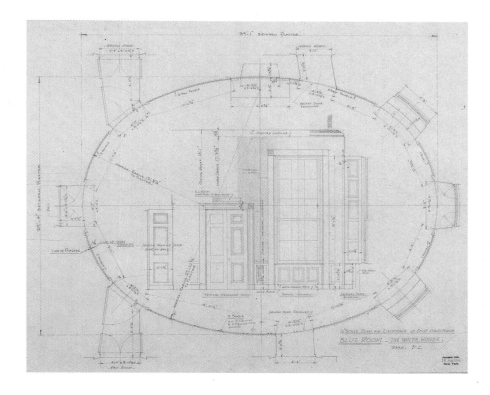

Wrightsman, and Boudin to see each proposal in the context of the architecture and furnishings of the room; the three model windows had open panes to allow the various schemes to be viewed by simulated daylight. Fascinated by this miniature room and all that it conveyed with regard to Jansen's dedication to detail, Jacqueline Kennedy became further enamored of Stéphane Boudin's skill as a designer. (In 1980, during a rare interview to defend Boudin's contributions to the project, the former First Lady began by noting that when "you saw him work, you saw what no American decorator could do. In France you are trained as an interior architect.")[11]

Boudin's proposal for the treatment of the walls of the Blue Room was in distinct contrast to that selected during the Truman renovation and which Boudin himself temporarily utilized for nearly two years. (The ca. 1952 Schumacher-manufactured deep blue silk with repeating gold urns with flowers appeared too harsh to Boudin. Prior to installing his choice, the Frenchman softened the existing wall hangings with large portraits of George Washington and John Quincy Adams as well as with a pair of elongated Adam-style looking glasses.) From perhaps his first visit to the White House in February 1961, Stéphane Boudin envisioned the oval-shaped Blue Room as

Transitional stage in the decoration of the Blue Room showing original and reproduction Bellangé armchairs and the Truman-era wall covering. Courtesy John F. Kennedy Library.

a tent room like that created for Napoleon's Malmaison by Charles Percier and Pierre-François-Léonard Fontaine. Stripes were selected for the walls, with a fabric valance to encircle the room below the cornice. Originally Boudin was encouraged to work with walls of blue. "It will be a blue silk," described Janet G. Felton, Secretary to the Fine Arts Committee, "alternating dull and satin stripes, with plain blue for the festoons around the cornice."[12] However, a proposal was soon made to change the coloring of the walls to white-on-white. Cream or white walls had evidently existed in the room during the administration of James Madison (1809–17), and this fact certainly aided Boudin's argument that white walls provided a more pleasing transition between the flanking Green and Red rooms.

The use of a continuous valance encircling a room was both a favorite theme of Boudin's and a period treatment associated with a number of famous early-nineteenth-century interiors, including that of the White House. Boudin had used a continuous valance in the Yellow Drawing Room of Leeds Castle. This treatment softened the contrasting proportions of a monumental Georgian cornice and an equally imposing mantel with the more delicate furniture in the room. For the White House Blue Room, the continuous valance performed a somewhat similar function. The total number of interruptions to the elliptical walls of the room is nine (five doorways, three windows, and a fireplace). Boudin's continuous valance unified the room, joining eight uneven spans of wall.

Period documents served as the Frenchman's foundation for the Blue Room redecoration. Interior decorator Mark Hampton, in his 1992 book *Legendary Decorators of the Twentieth Century,* attributed Boudin's Blue Room scheme to the Music Room of the Residenz München (Munich). Indeed, that early-nineteenth-century interior did include striped satin walls with a continuous valance. (Hampton's editor for the book was Jacqueline Kennedy Onassis. Possibly she shared Boudin's source of inspiration with Hampton while he prepared the text.) Similar wall treatments are visible in two other period sources that were familiar to Stéphane Boudin. The first is a painting depicting a Parisian evening of cards by Jean-François Bosio, which is in the Bibliothèque Nationale, Cabinet des Estampes, Paris. Equally possible as a source for inspiration—especially with the knowledge that Boudin originally proposed blue-on-blue striped walls—is Englishman Robert Smirke's 1798 watercolor of Charles Percier's decoration of Madame Récamier's bedroom, which included blue walls capped by a cream-colored valance.

Literally closer to home, a surviving account of Benjamin Henry Latrobe's decoration of Dolley Madison's parlor in the White House includes the following description of a similar treatment, albeit not in blue: the draperies "in the room were made of sunflower yellow damask with a valance of swags and draperies topping each window. The valance continued all around the top of the room, the stiff festoons looping up to a pole placed near the ceiling line. . . ."[13]

Evening of Cards *by Jean-François Bosio, early nineteenth century. Courtesy Collection of the Bibliothèque Nationale, Cabinet des Estampes, Paris.*

It is not known if Boudin referred to the period account of Latrobe's design. The description was included in Ethel Lewis's 1937 history of the mansion, *The White House.* Jacqueline Kennedy may have been made aware of this book while researching the history of the mansion and its furnishings prior to moving in. Certainly the discovery of the Monroe pier table through an obscure fifteen-year-old magazine article suggests the variety of resources explored by the First Lady. However, even if Latrobe's design for Mrs. Madison's parlor was familiar to Boudin, it could not have served as a primary source for his concept of a continuous valance for the Blue Room. Latrobe's valance was no doubt in the more delicate English Regency style he preferred. Boudin's valance was more substantial and quite close to the French Empire documents previously noted; there were no swags or poles like those used by Latrobe.

Satisfying Jacqueline Kennedy's concern that only American textiles be used for the redecoration of the Blue Room, Jansen's New York office ordered the silk for the walls, windows, and continuous valance from Scalamandré. The walls were covered in a cream-on-cream silk stripe while the drapery and valance panels were made of a light-blue silk taffeta. An additional order for specially dyed blue velvet for a cloth for the center table was also placed with the New York–based firm. All of these textiles were donated to the project by Franco Scalamandré.

The fabric for the upholstery of the gilt chairs proved more complex. Boudin reviewed collections of period textiles in Paris before deciding on his

ABOVE: *Robert Smirke's 1798 watercolor of Madame Récamier's bedroom designed by Charles Percier. Stéphane Boudin was familiar with this design, which is similar to his own proposal for the White House Blue Room. Courtesy Royal Institute of British Architects, London.*

RIGHT: *Published photograph of original painting by F. Bayerlein of Music Room, Munich Palace. Interior designer Mark Hampton believes this was the inspiration for the White House Blue Room. Courtesy Mark Hampton.*

first proposal, an Empire floral motif for the chair back and a medallion for the seat. A drawing from Paris was forwarded to the First Lady. Subsequently the drawing was directed to Franco Scalamandré, whose success with reproducing Boudin's previously submitted Red Room documents assured his involvement in this next chapter of the restoration project. ("Mrs. Kennedy was delighted to hear that you will make the material for the Blue Room," wrote Janet G. Felton to the textile manufacturer in early 1962. She continued by noting that "more documents have survived for the Blue Room than any other room in the White House. . . . Mrs. Kennedy will forward the designs to you as soon as possible.")[14]

RIGHT: *Blue Room prior to its complete redecoration, December 1962. Courtesy John F. Kennedy Library.*

FACING PAGE: *President Kennedy during a presentation ceremony in the completed Blue Room, April 18, 1963. Courtesy John F. Kennedy Library.*

While formulating a sample of this first proposal, the White House curator told Mrs. Kennedy about a portrait of James Monroe at New York's City Hall that included the original upholstery for the gilt suite in the background. Scalamandré went to study the crimson upholstery recorded by artist John Vanderlyn and noted the gold eagle clutching a cluster of arrows, surrounded by a laurel wreath. By May Boudin's original pattern was scrapped. Jayne Wrightsman wrote to assure Franco Scalamandré that "Mr. Boudin has told me that it [the fabric] will be very pretty with the eagle."[15] However, changes were still to be made. In an August memorandum to the First Lady, William Elder asked about the color of the fabric: "Janet wanted me to check with you on the material for the . . . chairs. The original design [Boudin's first proposal] . . . was white on blue. Since the design is now to be an eagle in a wreath . . . do you want the eagle to be white, or the two tones of gold as in the original Monroe design?"[16] No doubt Boudin recommended the change from gold to white to coincide with his plans for white stripes and a blue valance for the walls. The decorator provided a period sample of a white-on-

blue silk lampas featuring an eagle surrounded by a laurel wreath, and a matching seat medallion. The pattern of the sample was similar to that in the Monroe portrait, although Boudin's document had an eagle clutching lightning bolts instead of arrows.

In August 1962 Elder wrote to a vacationing Jacqueline Kennedy that the sample from Scalamandré had arrived. "As you can see," noted the Curator to the First Lady, "the eagle for the chair back looks more like a plucked chicken and the weaving is very coarse."[17] This sample was an adaptation of the rather crudely painted Monroe upholstery in the Vanderlyn portrait and, as Elder's assessment might suggest, it did not receive White House approval. From Ravello, Italy, the First Lady expressed a similar feeling about the submitted sample, noting that she was disappointed by its rough texture and color.[18] By September Boudin provided Scalamandré with his document—a white eagle grasping a cluster of lightning bolts on blue field. Scalamandré wrote to Jacqueline Kennedy that he was pleased the first eagle sample had not been accepted and that he believed Boudin's period textile would lead to a beautiful fabric for the chairs. However, the second sample also does not seem to have met Mrs. Kennedy's expectations. In a September 20, 1962, handwritten letter to Henry du Pont, the First Lady expressed great disappointment with the recent American-manufactured textile samples. By the end of September Boudin was instructed to find another manufacturer for the upholstery fabric.

In all fairness to Scalamandré, it is possible that Jacqueline Kennedy's "disappointment" with his final sample also had to do with her anger over the series of articles on the restoration project written by Maxine Cheshire. The *Washington Post* columnist talked her way into the inner sanctums of a number of suppliers to the restoration project, including Jansen's New York offices and the textile mill of Franco Scalamandré. Believing that Cheshire had White House permission to write the articles, including one entitled "They never introduce M. Boudin," Scalamandré proudly showed the eagle fabric that was set on the loom. He was no doubt more enthusiastic than the First Lady would have liked, and his relationship with the Kennedy White House was greatly changed as a result.

The Parisian firm of Tassinari and Châtel was Boudin's choice to succeed Scalamandré. Since the mid-eighteenth century the firm had produced

President and Mrs. Kennedy receiving guests in the restored Blue Room, February 12, 1963. Courtesy John F. Kennedy Library.

silks and trimmings for most of the great palaces of Europe. Tassinari and Châtel, noted a 1962 article, still "possesses the collections, the records, the cartoons and the looms, thanks to which it can resume all the ancient manufactures."[19] Boudin incorporated their fabrics in both contemporary and historical projects throughout his career. Yet, with American sensitivity to foreign products being used in the White House, Boudin had often been directed away from his preferred fabric source. Perhaps justifying the decision with the fact that the original Monroe upholstery fabric had been manufactured in France, Tassinari and Châtel received the commission to manufacture the eagle fabric for the Blue Room.

This selection of a non-American manufacturer immediately brought about new problems. To protect the White House from negative publicity regarding the purchase of foreign materials, Jansen, not the White House, placed the actual order with Tassinari and Châtel. Once completed, the fabric was shipped to the U.S. Embassy in Paris. From there the silk was sent to the Department of State in Washington, D.C., and then to the White House.

(Because there had been so many delays in agreeing on a manufacturer, it was found impossible to have the eagle fabric ready for the room's January 1963 public unveiling. Franco Scalamandré donated additional yardage of the solid blue taffeta used to make the draperies and valance for the temporary upholstery of the Monroe chairs despite his anger that a foreign manufacturer had taken over the production of the eagle fabric.)

In uniting the furniture with the architecture of the Blue Room, Stéphane Boudin designed a white and gold treatment for the dado and cornice. This was inspired by the white marble and gilt-bronze Louis XVI–style mantel designed for the room by Charles McKim in 1902. Completed as a gift to the project by New York society painter and craftsman Peter Guertler, the scheme helped to soften the contrast between the striking gilded suite of Monroe furniture and the starkness of the white walls, dado, and ceiling.

Additional furnishings were obtained for the room under the watchful eye of Boudin. The White House acquired three portraits, painted from life, of Thomas Jefferson, James Monroe, and Andrew Jackson. These were joined by existing copies of life portraits of George Washington, John Adams, James Madison, and John Quincy Adams, to create a gallery of the nation's first seven presidents. Boudin displayed four of these portraits below a set of French Empire black and gilt sconces that were placed on the piers between the windows and doors of the room. This hanging of paintings below sconces was a Boudin trademark. He incorporated a similar treatment in Lady Baillie's bedroom at Leeds Castle as well as in a transitional decorative stage of the White House Red Room.

Lighting was provided by an exceptional French Empire crystal and gilt-bronze chandelier. Boudin must have personally selected the chandelier and sconces for the room because they were almost identical to those used in the Music Room of the Residenz München, the early-nineteenth-century interior that Mark Hampton credited as Boudin's inspiration for the Blue Room. Other additions to the room included a fine pair of caryatid-base torchères, an early-nineteenth-century Savonnerie carpet in shades of pink, blue, and gold, and a pair of French gilt-bronze chenets for the fireplace.

As for Henry du Pont's reaction to the completed Blue Room, it has often been reported that he was shocked and dismayed by the Frenchman's interpretation of the celebrated salon. J. B. West even recalled that du Pont could be heard muttering his disdain for the room every time he passed through its doors. Whatever truth there may be in such statements, du Pont publicly supported the redecoration of the room as well as its benefactors. He wrote to Jayne Wrightsman in January 1963, specifically commenting on the success of the Blue Room. Ever the diplomat, he praised the room, but not vigorously, saying that the colors were "quite perfect and different."[20]

Boudin's finished product was not unlike a formal reception room in a European palace. It was also not unlike the type of room President James Monroe attempted to create in the early nineteenth century using his numerous French purchases. The Bellangé furniture was placed around the perimeter of the room, while a table, draped in blue velvet, was positioned in the center. After Boudin's redecoration the room did have the "sense of . . . ceremony" that Jacqueline Kennedy sought for it.[21]

The Ground Floor

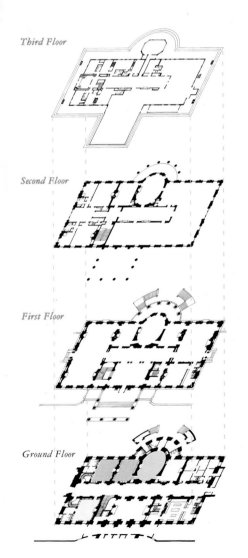

Third Floor

Second Floor

First Floor

Ground Floor

When the Kennedys entered the White House, the ground floor of the mansion was as it had been designed for Theodore Roosevelt by McKim, Mead, and White in 1902. The Beaux-Arts architectural firm had converted a dark, damp basement into a series of small reception and receiving rooms. This reconfiguration had been dictated by changes in State dinner procedures whereby the majority of guests arrived at the new East Wing instead of the State floor's main entrance; once on the mansion's ground floor, guests used the newly created rooms as lounges for straightening ties and smoothing gowns before ascending the stairs to dinner.

In the following years, the McKim, Mead, and White design was further developed. In 1917 Edith Galt Wilson relocated the collection of presidential porcelain to one of these lounges, creating the China Room, and nearly twenty years later Franklin Roosevelt selected another for an official White House library. Harry S. Truman's ambitious 1948–1952 renovation of the entire house gave further prestige to the turn-of-the-century design of the ground floor. Four rooms, including the Library and China Room, were paneled in variations of eighteenth-century Georgian architecture made from salvaged White House timbers. The increased grandeur of these rooms was no doubt intended to have them serve as mini–State reception rooms. However, renovation cost overruns led to a piecemeal approach to their completion. Draperies from State Rooms were cut down for their smaller windows, while carpets and furniture were gathered from storage. These budget interiors were what

Jacqueline Kennedy inherited when she became First Lady, and their refurbishing is what both du Pont and Boudin saw as a priority for the restoration project.

THE DIPLOMATIC RECEPTION ROOM

A partial exception to the budget-conscious appearance of these rooms was the collection of American Federal furniture installed in the oval Diplomatic Reception Room in 1960 by the National Society of Interior Designers. An unsolicited gift during the Eisenhower administration, this group of chairs, tables, and a magnificent New York serpentine-shaped sofa immediately became the mansion's finest assemblage of period furniture. Recognizing that the terms of the gift kept the furniture from being relocated to the needier State floor, Jacqueline Kennedy and Henry du Pont sought to enhance the

RIGHT: *The Diplomatic Reception Room after the 1960 AIID redecoration. Courtesy John F. Kennedy Library.*

Diplomatic Reception Room itself. For an appropriate backdrop they selected a series of scenic wallpaper panels produced by the French manufacturer Zuber & Company in 1834. Entitled "Scenic America," the paper portrayed an idealized North American landscape featuring Virginia's Natural Bridge, Boston Harbor, and the United States Military Academy at West Point.

This wallpaper served as testament to Henry du Pont's importance to the Kennedy restoration. In 1961 the White House was offered for sale a set of wallpaper panels salvaged from a dilapidated house in Thurmont, Maryland. The White House purchased the paper for $12,500 from Washington preacher Peter Hill, who had originally obtained it for $50. This prompted Milton Glaser, President of the American Institute of Interior Designers, to claim that "somebody got stuck."[1] After pointing out that the wallpaper was still available new at a fraction of the cost paid for the original version, Glaser added: "Some people like broken things because they are old and broken down; maybe Mrs. Kennedy is one of them."[2] Such criticisms culminated in *Washington Post* columnist Maxine Cheshire's September 1962 series of articles on the extravagances of the project.

However strong the criticism from Glaser and members of the media, such remarks did not tarnish the reputation of the restoration, for behind the

BELOW: *The White House Library prior to the Kennedy administration, ca. 1960. Courtesy John F. Kennedy Library.*

FACING PAGE: *The restored White House Library, ca. 1962, showing one of the number of chandeliers temporarily placed in this room. Courtesy John F. Kennedy Library.*

choice of the period paper, as well as all other decisions, stood Henry Francis du Pont, the "expert." *Look* magazine noted in 1962, in reference to the new acquisition, that "while the wallpaper has created a stir, many people have overlooked the fact that the entire interior has been recreated and furnished with remarkable skill and distinction."[3] Du Pont provided that "skill and distinction."

THE LIBRARY

Henry du Pont's knowledge and reputation provided the direction for the refurbishing of the ground-floor Library, which was donated by the American Institute of Interior Designers. The Fine Arts Committee Chairman dictated the recreation of an early-nineteenth-century classical interior, and he ultimately approved of the AIID's alterations of the room's architecture. However, his initial decision was to create a late-eighteenth-century period interior based on the Georgian-style woodwork of the room.

After their initial walk-through, du Pont and the Curator of his Winterthur museum, John Sweeney, recommended that the room be furnished with Chippendale period furnishings to match the room's architecture. Du Pont quickly changed his mind, however, explaining to Mrs. Kennedy that "to my horror, on looking at Richard Howland's letter of April 10th, at the bottom of page three, the four lines, 'Thou Shalt Nots,' it seems quite certain that this house never had any furniture of the Chippendale period or earlier, Satinwood furniture, or French marquetry pieces. . . ."[4] The fact that the dates of the White House's original construction precluded the use of Chippendale period designs came into conflict with du Pont's own preference for that style, which was largely featured in the rooms of Winterthur. Rather than remove the historically inappropriate yet well-constructed woodwork, du Pont suggested "camouflaging" the Chippendale period feeling of the Library with paint. He described his decision to Cornelia Conger, a member of the AIID, saying, "I believe the best solution is to paint the Library which would disguise its period somewhat, and furnish it with 19th century furniture. Inasmuch as the architect erred in designing a Chippendale room, I think it would be unwise for us to follow suit. No one objected to having the Dining Room painted, therefore there is no reason why we should not paint the Library woodwork."[5]

Du Pont's recommendation for the treatment of the walls was adopted by the AIID, which proposed painting the paneling a pale yellow with high-lights picked out in ivory "to avoid too much emphasis on details in a room where numerous books create competing patterns."[6] After the implementation of the yellow and ivory scheme, a third color—antique gold—was subsequently introduced to provide a clearer distinction between the various planes of the paneling. This darker pigment may have been suggested by the First Lady or by Boudin, for it somewhat contradicted both du Pont's and the AIID's concerns about calling attention to the eighteenth-century quality of the paneling. Presumably selection of this new color was dictated by textiles already chosen for the room, such as the gold-on-ivory medallion-patterned fabric used for the window treatments. Architectural changes included a simplification of the overmantel, a reconfiguration of the applied moldings for storage space doors, and the installation of a mantelpiece from Salem, Massachusetts, with carving attributed to Samuel McIntire. To complete the period feel of the room, a more appropriate wood floor was placed on top of the Truman-era marble tiles.

Du Pont's suggestion of an early-nineteenth-century focus was closely adhered to as the Library project reached its next stage—the selection of furnishings. For the floor, the AIID acquired an exceptional green, ivory, and rose-colored French Aubusson carpet, on which was placed a ca. 1810 New York octagonal library table. Other furnishings assembled for the room included an extensive suite of caned seating furniture from the workshop of Duncan Phyfe as well as two mahogany lady's worktables, a pair of English Regency library chairs, and a New Hampshire lolling chair with double arm supports. From the ceiling was suspended a succession of chandeliers, the final one being a tole and crystal example once owned by James Fenimore Cooper, one of America's first internationally recognized authors.

For the walls, the Fine Arts Committee and its subcommittee for paintings acquired works representative of historic events. Over the mantel was placed *The Signing of the Declaration of Independence,* an oil sketch by nineteenth-century French artist Edouard Armand-Dumaresq. A significant example of how America's fight for independence served as a popular subject for artists of many nations, this sketch was probably based on the work of American artist John Trumbull. Elsewhere in the library were placed five portraits of native

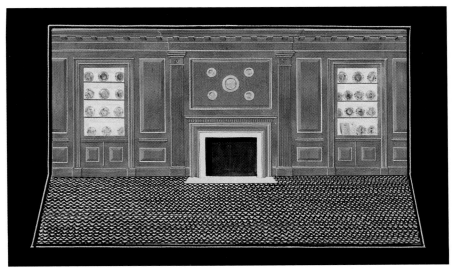

ABOVE: *Approved design for the Vermeil Room draperies, dated July 10, 1963. Courtesy Paul Manno. Photo: Jim Frank.*

ABOVE RIGHT: *Jansen's original proposal for the Vermeil Room, early 1963. Courtesy Paul Manno. Photo: Jim Frank.*

Americans painted by Charles Bird King on their 1821 visit to President James Monroe's White House. These rare portraits were found by actor and art connoisseur Vincent Price, who alerted the White House of their availability. The actual acquisition of the Native American images was made possible by Sears, Roebuck and Company, who underwrote the purchase in honor of their employees.

For filling the actual shelves of the library, President and Mrs. Kennedy appointed a committee of scholars that included Harvard's Lyman H. Butterfield, Princeton's Julian P. Boyd, and Kennedy advisor Arthur Schlesinger, Jr. Chaired by James T. Babb, Yale University's librarian, the committee's goal was defined as the compilation of books "most essential to the understanding of our National experience."[7] The Kennedys specifically desired a usable library rather than a collection of antique volumes—somewhat in contrast to the fine and decorative arts objects assembled for the room. Hence, the majority of books were recently published volumes, as opposed to first editions.

THE VERMEIL ROOM

The Vermeil Room, across the hall from the Library, was named for Mrs. Margaret Thompson Biddle's 1956 bequest of a fine collection of Renaissance to nineteenth-century English and French vermeil, or gilt silver. Although then–First Lady Mamie Eisenhower had relegated the collection to the room's series of built-in display cases, her successor began borrowing choice pieces for State Room tabletops in the first days of her husband's administration. Subsequently, vermeil montieth bowls, baskets, and wine coolers were used for the Flemish or informal floral arrangements developed by Jacqueline Kennedy and Rachel Lambert Mellon, a friend and self-trained horticulturist whose most famous contribution to the Kennedy White House was the planning and installation of the President's Rose Garden.

However, Jacqueline Kennedy did not utilize the entire Biddle bequest for flowers. The Vermeil Room still served as an exhibition gallery, and Stéphane Boudin began formulating its redecoration in early 1963. In that Boudin's reputation as one of the world's leading decorators developed through the acquisition of eighteenth-century paneled rooms as well as the training of craftsmen in the art of imitating their antique finishes, his proposal for the Vermeil Room must have come naturally. The Frenchman envisioned painting the room's paneled walls—boiserie—variations of blue and white, a favorite treatment he had previously adapted to the Paris dining room of the Duke and Duchess of Windsor, the Leeds Castle bedroom of Lady Olive Baillie, and the New York "Petit Salon [of] Mrs. Guest."[8]

But the painting of the Vermeil Room was just the beginning. "Our proposition has been accepted," noted Jansen's New York office in February 1963, "with the blue and white walls . . . white velvet in the vitrines, white damask drapes, and the white and blue carpet from Paris for the floor."[9] The draperies were trimmed in French-manufactured blue and off-white silk tassel fringe and hung from gilded brass rings and poles fitted with decorative finials. To this scheme Boudin directed the inclusion of one of two recently acquired early-nineteenth-century marble mantels with caryatid supports and a blue and gold chandelier. The last addition was a large center table draped in a specially dyed blue velvet, installed after Jacqueline Kennedy left the White House. Simple and sparse, Boudin's Vermeil Room was intended to serve as a museum exhibition gallery, with no furnishings standing between the visitor and the encased Biddle collection of vermeil along the walls. (This intent was further emphasized by Boudin's interest in adding to the number of built-in wall cases; he wanted to install one between the windows if structurally possible, which it proved not to be.)

*The China Room prior to the Kennedy adminis-
tration, ca. 1960. Courtesy John F. Kennedy
Library.*

THE CHINA ROOM

Stéphane Boudin's plans for the more familiar China Room next door followed
a similar path. The early 1963 proposal for this room consisted of "grey and
white walls, grey velvet drapes, red velvet to line the vitrines and the red and
snow flake rug from Stark for the floor."[10] The treatment for the room's single window consisted of straight-falling curtain panels of gray cotton velvet
capped by a matching stationary valance; all were trimmed in gray and red
silk moss fringe. The carpeting noted in the written proposal was actually
Boudin's second choice. In his first scheme he chose an ivory and red carpeting for installation wall to wall. Presumably Jacqueline Kennedy expressed
concern about so much white in the carpeting. Certainly Boudin's selection of
a white loop-pile floor covering for the second-floor Queen's Bedroom had
raised some concern about his understanding of the wear and tear of White
House rooms. The red-on-red Stark carpeting was no doubt seen as a more
practical choice. (A green version of this carpeting was selected for the well-
used main elevator.)

The proposed furnishing of the China Room illustrated Boudin's cre-
ativity as well as his flexibility in utilizing existing objects. From the beginning he appears to have been unhappy with the simple mantel surround

Jansen's original proposal for the China Room, early 1963. Courtesy Paul Manno. Photo: Jim Frank.

installed during the Truman administration. One proposal for its replacement called for walling over the fireplace and substituting a "marble console belonging to the White House."[11] Another proposal, slightly more eccentric in concept, called for replacing the simple surround with an "Empire mantelpiece with . . . two figures, . . . and using the other mantelpiece [eventually installed in the Vermeil Room] . . . as a console"[12] elsewhere in the room. The accepted solution was to simply utilize one of the marble mantels at the fireplace.

As he had for the Vermeil Room, Boudin suggested a single piece of furniture for the center of the China Room, but instead of a table he proposed a contemporary square banquette upholstered in the same gray cotton velvet as the draperies and trimmed with red silk cording and tassels. A history-conscious Jacqueline Kennedy expressed an interest in using the room's existing mid-

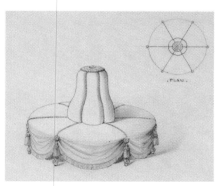

TOP: *Approved design for the China Room draperies, dated July 10, 1963. Courtesy Paul Manno. Photo: Jim Frank.*

BOTTOM: *Jansen's proposal for valance upholstery of the China Room "pouf." Courtesy Paul Manno. Photo: Jim Frank.*

nineteenth-century gilt-framed banquette, originally purchased for James Buchanan's Blue Room. She also wished to continue the use of red damask for the upholstery because it had become a "tradition."

Although this clearly was not what Boudin had intended for the China Room, he set about to fulfill, to some degree, the wishes of the First Lady. By October 1963 Jansen's New York office prepared a new upholstery proposal with a "design of valance for the low part of the [First Lady's chosen] round pouf."[13] This "valance"—a series of fabric swags—was a Boudin trademark incorporated in a famous suite of furniture for the Duchess of Windsor's Paris drawing room. Jansen's new proposal for the China Room banquette was assuredly intended to cover as much of the piece's gilt frame as possible, thus bringing it closer to what Boudin had originally proposed. However, it did not satisfy Jacqueline Kennedy's wish to show off the banquette's historical importance. Indeed, the proposal nearly masked all hints of its identity. Forging a compromise with the "master," the First Lady agreed to Boudin's proposed use of velvet instead of damask, but she chose to continue the traditional red color as well as the existing amount of upholstery coverage for the "pouf."

The change in upholstery color from gray made the China Room's only piece of furniture an extension of the red carpet as opposed to a much-needed contrast to it. Visually, the First Lady's selection segregated the light walls from the center of the room. She acknowledged this problem and accepted that a new carpet would have to be found to accomodate the use of red on the Buchanan banquette. However, she left the White House before this correction could be made.

The ground-floor reception rooms illustrated the differences between the respective philosophies of Henry du Pont and Stéphane Boudin. The Diplomatic Reception Room and Library more or less followed du Pont's preference for period room recreations where the assembled antiques corresponded with the period represented by the art, architecture, and textiles of the room. In contrast, the Vermeil and China rooms reflected Boudin's concern for proportion, balance, and, most important, what Jacqueline Kennedy described as "ceremony."[14] They were not intended as period rooms but as attractive spaces for the reception of guests.

Halls

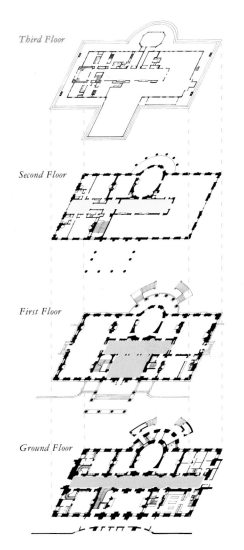

Third Floor

Second Floor

First Floor

Ground Floor

The halls of the White House are not of a scale that would allow them to be seen simply as connectors of rooms. With widths as great as eighteen feet, these spaces have a monumentality that requires treatment more as reception rooms than as passageways. Previous residents of the White House had used some of the mansion's halls as extended sitting areas; the Kennedys addressed the halls of each of the three floors in a different manner. For the ground floor, the focus was a museum-like arrangement of furniture and art representative of the nation's—and more specifically the White House's—history. For the main or State floor, the entrance and cross-halls mirrored those of Napoleon's Malmaison outside of Paris. And for the family floor, the East, West, and Center halls were arranged as three unique rooms intended partially as infor-mal reception areas and also as galleries of art and antiques. As with so much of the Kennedy restoration, the decoration of these spaces was a combined effort of many players. Henry du Pont, Sister Parish, and Stéphane Boudin were each influential in the formulation of decorative schemes. By the end of 1963, Boudin's contributions were the most visible.

THE GROUND FLOOR

When the Kennedys arrived at the White House, the ground-floor hallway that connected the Library, China Room, Vermeil Room, and Diplomatic Reception Room was sparsely furnished. The architecture reflected the plan of the house's original designer, James Hoban—particularly the ceiling's

PAGE 132: *Entrance Hall of the White House looking toward the Cross Hall. Visible are the McKim, Mead, and White torchères in the first stage of alteration as well as the pair of French Empire banquettes given by C .Z. Guest. Courtesy John F. Kennedy Library.*

BELOW: *Ground-floor corridor of the White House showing the placement of sculpture and pier tables as well as Henry du Pont's lighting fixtures, March 1962. Courtesy John F. Kennedy Library.*

impressive series of cross-vaults—but with marble walls and floors dating from the Truman era and few furnishings outside of potted palms, upholstered benches, and hospital-green carpets, the space was antiseptic in its overall appearance. The First Lady described it as looking like a "dentist's office bomb shelter."[1]

In planning for the redecoration of this hall, Jacqueline Kennedy and Henry du Pont assessed how the space was used on a daily basis. First and foremost, they recognized it as the corridor in which public visitors to the White House began their tour. They also acknowledged that it served as a passageway for guests to State functions in their progression to the main floor. A plan was subsequently devised to furnish the space in a variety of styles that would represent the evolution of decorative taste and artistic achievement in the United States. Thus, early-nineteenth-century New York pier tables, one

The east colonnade, which serves as the public entrance to the White House, shows the interpretative panels prepared at the suggestion of Jacqueline Kennedy, with frames designed by Stéphane Boudin. Courtesy John F. Kennedy Library.

labeled by Charles-Honoré Lannuier and the other attributed to him, were at home near a small Victorian settee and two chairs, 1862 wedding gifts to Mr. and Mrs. John de Witt from President and Mrs. Abraham Lincoln. Numerous other articles were added to the hall, including another pier table with a documented White House history, attributed to the workshop of Duncan Phyfe; an early-twentieth-century Frederick Remington bronze entitled *Coming Through the Rye;* and a late-eighteenth-century marble bust of Charles Hector, Count d'Estaing, commander of the French naval forces sent to aid in the American Revolution.

For this new gallery of American history Henry du Pont assembled a series of eleven English Regency–style lanterns and chandeliers. Replacing what could only be classified as common office fixtures, du Pont's acquisitions gave the long hall a sense of importance. With their delicate glass bells, brass anthemion ornaments, and fine chain supports, they also corrected the low, squat illusion imposed by the vaulted ceiling and three-quarter polished stone walls. Jacqueline Kennedy was greatly impressed with this transformation. In her last letter to du Pont as First Lady she observed that "to me, they do more than anything to give the feeling of an historic house—as it is here everyone comes in."[2]

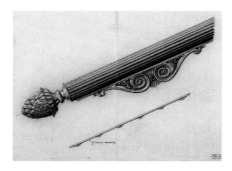

Jansen's proposal for handrail at stairwell connecting ground and State floors. Courtesy Paul Manno. Photo: Jim Frank.

Stéphane Boudin made numerous suggestions for this hall. The varnished pine doors leading to the ground-floor rooms were painted white following his directive. Boudin encouraged the replacement of the green cut-pile carpeting with a more regal red example and changed the upholstery of some of the furniture; the green velvet selected for the previously noted Victorian suite by one of the donors, Sister Parish herself, was recovered in "10 yards of red on rouge stripe."[3] He also designed the pedestals for two bronze standing figures representing nineteenth-century American statesmen Daniel Webster and Henry Clay.

Perhaps surprising is the fact that not all of Boudin's plans for the ground-floor hall were carried out. For the replacement of the main stair's existing stock handrail, Jansen sent Jacqueline Kennedy drawings of a two-inch fluted gilt rail with stylized acanthus leaf supports and finials. A February 1963 memorandum from Jansen's New York office noted the "design . . . has been accepted by Mrs. Kennedy. . . . Send estimate . . . for making the new hand rail on either side of the stairway and the existing middle . . . rail and posts will remain as they are, but will be gilded to match the new stairway."[4] It is likely that the estimate of $10,875, which included supplying "a temporary center metal hand rail while the existing [center] one is being gilded,"[5] was seen as exorbitant when the First Lady considered that the elaborate window draperies and bed hangings for the recently redecorated Queen's Bedroom together had cost just more than half as much. Far from a priority, the plans for the stairs leading to the State floor were postponed.

THE STATE FLOOR

In contrast to the melange of periods represented in the ground-floor hall, the furnishings for the State-floor Entrance Hall and Cross Hall were intended to represent the Empire style of the early nineteenth century. In part, this focus was dictated by the architecture of these classically inspired spaces, composed by McKim, Mead, and White in 1902 and enhanced during the Truman renovation of 1948–1952. Although Henry du Pont had definite ideas about these spaces, it was Stéphane Boudin's familiarity with early-nineteenth-century French palaces that led the decoration process.

To educate the First Lady in what "should" be done, Boudin no doubt recommended that she examine firsthand the entrance hall of Napoleon and

Josephine's Malmaison during the scheduled April 1961 State visit to Paris. France's Minister of Culture André Malraux arranged this side trip, personally escorting Jacqueline Kennedy through the restored palace where she "admired the beautiful First Empire furniture and decor, which were in keeping, in period and elegance, with the plans for the restoration of the White House. . . ."[6] In particular, she must have appreciated the restraint of color and the balance and proportion demonstrated in the decoration of Malmaison's entrance hall, which, in scale and intended use, was not unlike that of the White House. Upon her return to Washington, the First Lady acknowledged that both the Cross Hall and Entrance Hall, which served as backdrops for ceremonial processions, should have the same sense of importance as Malmaison's hall.

For the furnishing of the Cross Hall, Boudin and Mrs. Kennedy used the white and gold Empire-style chairs designed by Charles McKim for Theodore Roosevelt's Blue Room. Although du Pont saw this suite as unsuit-

RIGHT: *Renderings showing design history for State-floor hall torchères. From left to right: (a) original 1903 design with flower-like shades; (b) 1931 installation with flame-shaped electric lightbulbs; (c) 1961 Kennedy replacement with electrified faux candles; (d) 1963 Kennedy alteration using Empire-style cap with eight separate extended arms—from the center, beneath a bronze flame finial, indirect up-lighting is provided. Drawing by Robert Bentley Adams AIA.*

FACING PAGE: *Entrance Hall of the White House in December 1962, showing the official White House Christmas tree. The ongoing redecoration of the Blue Room prevented the tree being placed in its traditional location in that room. Courtesy John F. Kennedy Library.*

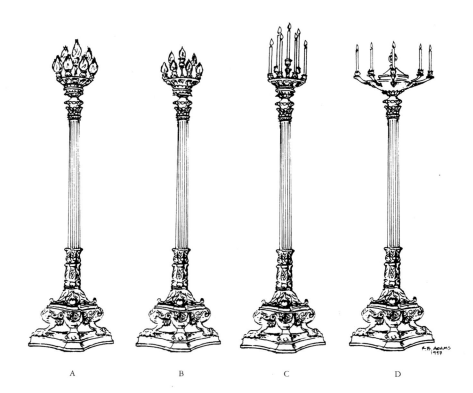

A   B   C   D

able for the White House because of its large scale, Boudin deemed the chairs ideal for the marble-floored hall that connected the East Room and State Dining Room. The four armchairs were placed along the south wall, while the two side chairs were positioned on the north wall at either end of a French Empire table once belonging to Napoleon's brother Joseph Bonaparte (this table was on loan from the Philadelphia Museum of Art). For the opposite end of the hall, two additional side chairs were commissioned for similar placement next to another pier table. Boudin's contemplation of refinishing the entire suite, perhaps to match the Bonaparte table, is revealed in a memorandum written to J. B. West, the mansion's Chief Usher, by Jacqueline Kennedy: "Can you ask if the Blue Room chairs we are having copied for front Hall should be mahogany or white and gold like others—then tell copier. . . ."[7] The final decision was to leave the chairs white and gold, and they were upholstered in crimson leather with gilt brass nail heads.

The ten McKim, Mead, and White-designed gilt bronze light standards, or torchères, that had adorned both the Cross Hall and Entrance Hall since 1902 were also subject to alteration. In a first go-around, Boudin suggested extending the torchères' three tiers of sockets with faux white candles

President and Mrs. Kennedy greeting visitors in the State floor's Cross Hall in February 1963. Behind the President is the portrait of Lafayette by the French painter Jean Heinsius. Courtesy John F. Kennedy Library.

lighted with small, flame-like electric bulbs. This was done, and although it helped to unite the heavier torchères with the more delicate pair of crystal chandeliers in the Cross Hall, the alteration did not satisfy Stéphane Boudin's eye for balance. Subsequently Jansen devised a wider gilt-bronze termination for the tops of the torchères where the new candles rose not from the central shaft but from eight separately extended arms.

For the Entrance Hall, Jansen's New York office found a pair of French Empire banquettes with elaborate gilt-bronze mounts and carved swans capping the arms. Superb examples of the Napoleonic era's preference for archaeologically correct furniture design, these Roman-inspired pieces were officially presented to the White House by socialite C. Z. Guest. They were upholstered by the New York firm of La Cava in a crimson leather similar to that used for the chairs in the Cross Hall, with the addition of a tooled gilt border framing the seat and back cushions. These banquettes—which Henry du Pont had viewed in New York and subsequently suggested for placement in the Cross Hall or "either between the windows or in the side windows"[8] of the Blue Room—complemented the austere screen of six Doric columns separating the two State-floor halls while they introduced regal red color to the otherwise off-white and buff palette of the Entrance Hall's architecture.

It is important to note that Henry du Pont's ideas for the Entrance and Cross halls were not completely dissimilar from those of Boudin. He too favored an Empire theme for these impressive spaces, although on a less monumental scale. Prior to the implementation of Boudin's plan, du Pont placed the previously noted pier tables in the Entrance Hall on either side of the screen of columns. He also added an important American card table given by Catherine Bohlen, who had recently presented an original Monroe gilt armchair for inclusion in the Blue Room. Boudin's dissatisfaction with this arrangement, particularly the placement of a drawing room card table in such a large space as the Entrance Hall, was expressed when he next arrived at the White House. A December 1961 memorandum to du Pont from the White House curator described disappointment in Boudin's subsequent rearrangement of the halls—specifically the removal of the card table and the relocation of the pier tables to the Cross Hall.

Du Pont had greater say in the selection and arrangement of art in the State-floor halls. Both he and the First Lady agreed that whatever was to be displayed within the Cross Hall should represent eighteenth- and nineteenth-century history, with no inclusion of twentieth-century works. From Virginia collector John Ryan they borrowed Charles Peale Polk's portrait of George Washington, Samuel F. B. Morse's likeness of Revolutionary War hero General John Stark, Chester Harding's *Charles Carroll of Carrollton*, and Gilbert Stuart's portrait of American naval commander John Barry. An equally important image of Lafayette by French court painter Heinsius was also placed on view. Added to the painted images were busts of Washington and Columbus, and, later, a magnificent 1804 bust of American Joel Barlow by premier French sculptor Jean-Antoine Houdon. In the Entrance Hall were placed the larger portraits of nineteenth-century Presidents Martin Van Buren and Andrew Jackson.

The hanging of portraits in the White House was not as simple as matching a subject of the appropriate historical period with an open wall space. Consideration had to be given to the political ramifications of selecting one President or other public official over another. The sensitive nature of this aspect of the restoration is illustrated in a memorandum from Curator William Elder to Jacqueline Kennedy in response to the display of the portraits of Chester Arthur, James Garfield, and Rutherford Hayes in the West Lobby. Apparently members of the press, attentive to the decorative changes taking place in the White House, printed a negative reaction to the lack of Democrats exhibited. Elder described his surprise at the attention, saying, "the portraits have been hung there because of their size with no political connotation for nearly seventy-five years, but . . . [Presidential aide Kenny] O'Donnell insisted one come down and that we hang two Democrats."[9] The fact that the all-Republican arrangement had gone unnoticed for such a period of time suggests that in addition to improving the appearance of the White House, the Kennedy restoration created a new awareness of the importance of objects in interpreting American history—or at least the importance of a bipartisan approach. (It is interesting that no criticism arose over the domination of the mansion's Entrance Hall by two Democrats, Van Buren and Jackson.)

To further enhance the State-floor halls, the First Lady directed the inclusion of ornamental plants. Although potted palms had been mainstays of recent administrations, Jacqueline Kennedy sought more interesting greenery. Among the chosen plants were five-foot-tall ficus trees, which were individually maintained and sculpted by the National Park Service. Placed in French-style garden boxes, these plants added interest to the screen of columns separating the State-floor halls and, when moved out onto the north portico, formed an attractive backdrop for the welcoming of official guests.

THE SECOND FLOOR

The second-floor hallways were treated to a far more contemporary look than those of the State floor. Sister Parish created the original concepts for the West, East, and Center halls. The West Sitting Hall became the First Family's living room, the East Sitting Hall a repository of furniture and memorabilia associated with the life of President James Monroe, and the Center Hall, the largest of the three, a gallery of American painting divided

into individual seating areas. Inevitably, du Pont influenced the acquisition of American antiques for all three spaces while Stéphane Boudin dictated their arrangement.

To the East Sitting Hall, an area generally thought of as a common receiving room for the flanking Lincoln and Queen's bedrooms, Jacqueline Kennedy, Sister Parish, and Henry du Pont relocated pieces of reproduction and period furniture formerly used in the Monroe Room, which by then had been renamed the Treaty Room. Against an off-white carpet were positioned comfortable club chairs formerly in the Lincoln Bedroom, an American Empire sofa on which it was believed President James Monroe had died, and a series of reproductions of Monroe-owned pieces commissioned by Mrs. Herbert Hoover in the early 1930s. This selection of furniture and its subsequent arrangement clearly defined the East Sitting Hall—which also became known as the Monroe Hall—as an attractive passage for those entering or leaving the bedrooms, and little more.

For this intentionally uninviting space, Stéphane Boudin adapted principles of landscape design for dramatic effect. In mid-1961 the Frenchman replaced the existing box-like window treatment with an elaborate design of green and off-white silks that followed the form of the large lunette window; the arc of green fabric was manipulated in such a way as to create a series of evenly spaced stationary swags, while the off-white taffeta undercurtains served the more utilitarian function of softening the flow of light. To complete his intended scheme, Boudin placed a Monroe tri-columnar-based table in front of the window. Together the theater-like drapery treatment and the table formed an attractive focal point noticeable from the opposite end of the second floor. In fact, one could not help but be visually drawn through the succession of doorways to the silhouette of the architectural

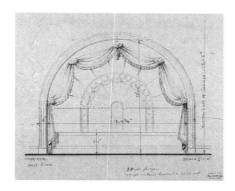

ABOVE: *Jansen's June 13, 1961, design of the window treatment for the East and West sitting halls' lunette windows. Courtesy Paul Manno. Photo: Jim Frank.*

BELOW: *East Sitting Hall or Monroe Hall, May 1962, showing Boudin's elaborate window treatment with Monroe table in front. Courtesy John F. Kennedy Library.*

table, which read as a great garden folly or temple framed by an alley of trees.

Certainly the Center Hall of the second floor was more inviting. In the largest room on the second floor Sister Parish arranged numerous sofas and chairs in small, intimate seating areas. Walls and carpeting were off-white. Upholstery fabrics were also kept light, ranging from white silk damask to green-on-white brocade. At the east end of the room, flanking the doors to the grand staircase, Jacqueline Kennedy placed two halves of a Chinese coromandel screen. A baby grand piano belonging to President Truman as well as a fine Philadelphia chair-back settee and two of four matching armchairs were positioned nearby along the south wall of the room. The rare suite of seating furniture was donated to the Fine Arts Committee by Mr. and Mrs. Adolph Henry Meyer through their Americana Foundation.

An equally important acquisition was a serpentine-shaped Federal sofa with an elaborately carved floral crest attributed to Salem, Massachusetts, craftsman Samuel McIntire. Placed just to the right of the entrance to the Yellow Oval Room, this sofa served as the central focus of the main seating area. Next to the sofa stood a pair of comfortable club chairs and two of a set

LEFT: *The second-floor Center Hall, looking into the West Sitting Hall, 1962. Courtesy John F. Kennedy Library.*

ABOVE: *The second-floor Center Hall, April 1963, showing the breakfront donated by Jules Stein temporarily placed over the built-in bookcase. The divided coromanel screen can be seen at the far end of the room. Courtesy John F. Kennedy Library.*

of four late-eighteenth-century English Adam-style armchairs formerly used in the Red Room. Above this grouping was arranged part of an important series of twenty American Indian portraits by nineteenth-century artist George Catlin. Borrowed from the National Gallery of Art early in the restoration, these paintings remained among Jacqueline Kennedy's favorites.

Early in the project, Mr. and Mrs. Jules Stein offered to donate furniture toward the completion of one White House room. At Henry du Pont's suggestion the Steins chose the Center Hall as the focus of their donation. In a July 1961 letter to Jayne Wrightsman, du Pont mentioned a recent visit to the Steins, who, having already selected some furniture, sought the approval of the Fine Arts Committee chairman. Du Pont "assured [them] it would surely be accepted if it were Sheraton, Hepplewhite, or Adams [*sic*]."[10] Continuing with his letter, du Pont noted his explanation to the Steins of plans for the Cross Hall, including the idea that the "big shells over some of the doors . . . [were

West Sitting Hall looking toward lunette win-
dow, late 1961. Mrs. Kennedy's Empire-style
desk, formerly belonging to her father, is shown
at the left of the photo. Across the room is the
eighteenth-century commode given to her by
French President Charles de Gaulle. Courtesy
John F. Kennedy Library.

to] be suppressed"[11] as well as Mr. Stein's suggestion that big mahogany breakfronts be placed in front of the existing built-in bookcases along the north wall. Indeed, for a brief time, a large secretary did cover one of the cases. However, this massive piece of furniture more than dwarfed the other furnishings as well as the overall architecture of the room, and it was soon removed.

For the West Sitting Hall, Sister Parish planned a reinstallation of the Kennedys' Georgetown living room. She ordered the construction of two built-in bookcases for the northeastern and southeastern corners of the room for the First Lady's collection of art books, as well as the painting of the room the now familiar off-white. Along the south wall was positioned Jacqueline Kennedy's most prized possession—her father's Empire-style slant-front desk. The First Lady, noted the mansion's chief usher, "worried more about scratches-in-transit, or [this desk's] . . . improper care, than about any other piece of furniture or art in the White House or in her own house."[12] From this desk she orchestrated much of the restoration project.

For comfort, Parish and the First Lady devised a conversation group in front of the hall's great lunette window. A fully tufted sofa, club chairs, a Lawson-style loveseat, and one of a pair of wing chairs formed the nucleus of the room. Installed underneath the coffee table was a small needlepoint carpet, one of Jacqueline Kennedy's first Jansen purchases, made while her husband was a senator. At the center of the room, behind the sofas and chairs, were positioned, in succession, a marble-topped table with a Monroe provenance (during the restoration this table was placed in the Blue Room, then the West Sitting Hall, and, finally, the East Sitting Hall), an Italian games table owned by the Kennedys, and, lastly, an eighteenth-century English partners' desk, which was part of the Stein gift for the Center Hall. Along the north wall stood an eighteenth-century mahogany commode presented to the First Lady by French President Charles de Gaulle, on which was proudly displayed a silver-framed photograph of the famous State dinner at Versailles.

West Sitting Hall, looking east, showing bookcases built for the Kennedys during Sister Parish's early 1961 decoration of the room.

Jacqueline Kennedy saying farewell to White House staff in the West Sitting Hall prior to her departure from the White House on December 6, 1963. After removing her personal items, Mrs. Kennedy rearranged some White House furnishings to cover bare spaces in an effort to make the house more welcoming to the Johnsons. Courtesy John F. Kennedy Library.

For the hall's window Parish devised a treatment of straight-falling curtain panels and a pleated valance made from the same multicolored printed cotton she had selected for upholstering the large sofa and slipcovering the wing chairs. Less than a year after their installation the Parish draperies were replaced with a duplicate of Boudin's dramatic green and off-white semicircular treatment for the East Sitting Hall.

In this room John and Jacqueline Kennedy entertained friends and family. Perhaps an evening began with cocktails in the Yellow Oval Room, then was followed by dinner in the President's Dining Room and conversation in the West Sitting Hall. Other evenings may have begun and ended in the more informal hall. Positioned in one corner was the President's personal bar, while in another was a stereo. Books on art and history were neatly stacked on the room's center table, which also held a large arrangement of flowers. On the smaller tables were current magazines, cigarette boxes, and a variety of family photographs. This was the room that was the least Presidential and, thus, it was the one preferred by the Kennedys during private evenings "at home."

The Private Dining Rooms

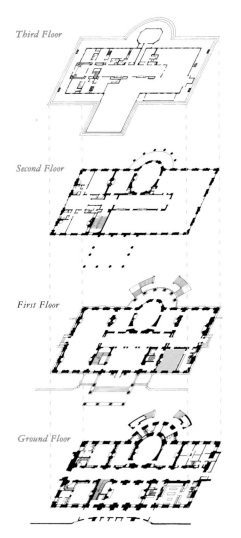

Third Floor

Second Floor

First Floor

Ground Floor

From November 1800, when John and Abigail Adams became the first residents, the White House had always had a separate dining room for the President and his family. Located on the main level of the mansion, the Family Dining Room served, until the Kennedy administration, as the one private chamber on the otherwise very public State floor. However, Jacqueline Kennedy soon deemed the grand scale of the State Rooms inappropriate for family gatherings. She subsequently sponsored the creation of a new private dining room on the second floor of the White House. In doing so, the First Lady defined the way all succeeding Presidential families have lived at 1600 Pennslyvannia Avenue.

THE PRESIDENT'S DINING ROOM

During the first weeks of the Kennedy administration, Jacqueline Kennedy worked with Sister Parish on a reformulation of the family quarters of the White House. After careful consideration of the room layout, the First Lady decided to convert the suite directly across the West Sitting Hall from her own to a dining room and small kitchen. Originally this transformation involved the duplication of the Kennedys' Georgetown dining room, which had been furnished in a casual translation of the Louis XVI style. Frenchman Stéphane Boudin advised on a general scheme for the room, including a rather simple design for window draperies. However, Henry du Pont and Sister Parish soon proposed a much more American scheme for this new dining space.

PAGE 152: *The completed President's Dining Room, July 1963. Courtesy John F. Kennedy Library.*

By late 1961 the Fine Arts Committee began acquiring examples of American Federal dining furniture for the room, the majority of which was paid for by Mr. and Mrs. Charles W. Engelhard of New Jersey. A side table attributed to late-eighteenth-century Annapolis cabinetmaker John Shaw was joined by a New England sideboard once owned by Daniel Webster. A Philadelphia mantel with a central tablet depicting the Battle of Lake Erie, dated 1817, was installed at the fireplace, while a combined group of antique and reproduction New York Sheraton-style dining chairs were placed about the period pedestal dining table.

For the room's two windows, Sister Parish and Henry du Pont devised asymmetrical treatments of blue silk trimmed in an elaborate green tassel fringe. Evidently the design was taken from one of du Pont's own early-nineteenth-century pattern books at Winterthur. It is possible that Stéphane Boudin also participated in the design of these draperies, although surely unbeknownst to the others. This is suggested in a September 19, 1962, letter to Parish, in which Jacqueline Kennedy herself ordered yardage of Brunschwig and Fils' blue taffeta (#5168) for the valances and jabots and additional yardage of a lighter blue taffeta for the drapery panels.[1] This mention of a lighter-colored material for the draperies, as opposed to that used for the valances, is similar to the First Lady's earlier translation of Boudin's scheme for the Yellow Oval Room draperies being fabricated at about the same time. In fact, Parish's response to the two-tone approach for the Oval Room seems to reveal an unfamiliarity with the concept, although she noted in her own letter to Mrs. Kennedy that "the undercurtain (drapery panel) material we can change to the paler [color]. . . ."[2] The finished dining room draperies were the most elaborate of the restoration project.

For the walls, du Pont directed the installation of "Scenes of the American Revolution," a later version of the 1834 "Scenic America" wallpaper already included in the ground-floor Diplomatic Reception Room. The incorporation of American and English soldiers in the familiar natural and urban scapes led Henry du Pont to deem the ca. 1853 French-manufactured paper an ideal addition to the White House collection. He closely monitored its installation, noting in a November 22, 1961, letter to Jayne Wrightsman that Peter Guertler was going to "add a little more decor to the paper over the mantelpiece in the Private Dining Room."[3] The paper's acquisition and sub-

Transitional view of the President's Dining Room, January 31, 1962. Courtesy John F. Kennedy Library.

sequent installation were paid for by one of Sister Parish's devoted clients, Brooke Astor.

Lighting fixtures and floor coverings seem to have been less easily decided on for this particular room. Two different Empire chandeliers were tried in the space before the First Lady settled on the installation of a late-eighteenth-century crystal chandelier that had originally been acquired for

Restored President's Dining Room on the second floor following the installation of the Zuber "Scenic America" wallpaper donated by Mrs. Vincent Astor. Behind the screen is the entrance to the newly created family kitchen. Courtesy John F. Kennedy Library.

the Green Room by Mrs. Calvin Coolidge. Jacqueline Kennedy, Sister Parish, and Stéphane Boudin had difficulty in finding carpets that were both attractive and durable. A Middle-Eastern rug from the White House collection was exchanged for a solid oyster-white area carpet. Fearing that whatever antique carpet that could be found would inevitably not hold up under the wear, Mrs. Kennedy approved Jansen's suggestion of a contemporary gold and off-white flame-stitch patterned carpet, which was installed in mid-1963.

Detail of the Family Dining Room showing temporary placement of newly acquired antique furniture, August 1961. Courtesy John F. Kennedy Library.

Durability was also a factor with regard to chair seat upholstery. The first selection for the Federal-style dining chairs had been an oyster-colored silk damask, presumably woven by the New York firm of Bergamo under Sister Parish's supervision. This fabric proved inappropriate for a dining room, and by early 1963 Jacqueline Kennedy turned to Jansen for a replacement material. Likely referring to the material he had selected for Lady Baillie's dining chairs at Leeds Castle, Boudin suggested white leather tooled in imitation of the more fragile silk damask. This was approved by the White House, and Jansen supplied leather for twenty side chairs and four armchairs after receiving templates from Chief Usher J. B. West.

THE FAMILY DINING ROOM

Of course, not all of these twenty-four chairs were for the second-floor President's Dining Room. Half of the chairs were intended for the Family Dining Room on the State floor, which during the Kennedy administration became a smaller official dining room for Presidential meetings and business breakfasts. The Family Dining Room was the strongest visual contribution of Fine Arts Committee members Sister Parish, who orchestrated its decoration, and Jane Engelhard, who, with her husband Charles, funded the actual transformation.

Parish's ability to find wealthy contributors for the White House restoration project was recognized by the First Lady, du Pont, and others. Upon learning of a mid-1961 threat to resign over Stéphane Boudin's ever-increasing participation in the restoration project, Jayne Wrightsman declared to Parish that she "must never think of resigning from the committee! It would break Jackie's heart + mine, too, I might add! The White House is so lucky to have you."[4] Such expressions of concern gave Parish an edge, allowing her to declare a degree of independence with rooms sponsored by personal friends or clients. Indeed, the redecoration of the Family Dining Room was the responsibility of Parish and her then-new partner, Albert Hadley, because the work was underwritten by the Engelhards, who were both friends and clients.

For the redecoration of the Family Dining Room, Sister Parish and Henry du Pont asked Robert Raley, consulting architect to Winterthur, to assess the architecture of the room. He proposed some modifications, while

Presidential business breakfast in the Family Dining Room, June 15, 1962. Originally intended as the family's private dining room, this room soon became a smaller State dining room upon the completion of the new President's Dining Room and kitchen on the second floor. Courtesy John F. Kennedy Library.

showing great respect for the neoclassical scheme originally conceived of by McKim, Mead, and White in 1902. Raley removed the series of wood moldings used to divide the upper portion of the walls into panels. He also devised permanent window valances—actual extensions of the wall—that reduced the interior height of the windows without altering their exterior appearance. This allowed the continuation of the existing cornice molding around the room, where before it had been interrupted by the two taller window openings. Per Jacqueline Kennedy's approval the walls were painted a bright yellow, with moldings and trim of white.

For the fireplace, Robert Raley worked with a number of proposals that together well illustrate the complicated processes inherent in the White

ABOVE: *"Carpet by others for Private Dining Room 1st Fl." Jansen, May 21, 1962. Courtesy Paul Manno. Photo: Jim Frank.*

RIGHT: *The Family Dining Room on the State floor, 1963, as decorated by Sister Parish. Courtesy White House Historical Association.*

House project. Raley and du Pont seem to have agreed that a recently installed Philadelphia wood mantel with a central tablet representing the Battle of Lake Erie should be replaced. (This mantel was transferred to the President's Dining Room on the second floor.) The restoration architect subsequently proposed the inclusion of an elaborate Federal-style mantel that he owned, the specific design of which is not known. However, Henry du Pont wanted to use an early-nineteenth-century English mantel that had been donated to the project by the English Speaking Union. (This mantel was one the First Lady hoped to include in the second-floor dining room and that Boudin later installed in the China Room.) The final choice was a dark-green and white marble mantel with a large eagle in the central tablet. Purchased

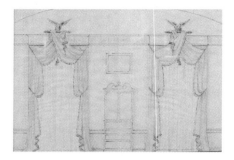

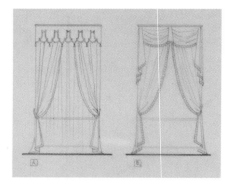

TOP: *Colored pencil sketch by Albert Hadley of English-inspired drapery proposal, ca. 1962. Courtesy Parish-Hadley, New York. Photo: Jim Frank.*

CENTER: *Colored pencil sketch by Albert Hadley of eagle-capped drapery proposal for Family Dining Room, ca. 1962. Courtesy Parish-Hadley, New York. Photo: Jim Frank.*

BOTTOM: *"Small Dining Room—First Floor." Drapery proposals for Family Dining Room submitted by Jansen in May 1962. Courtesy Paul Manno. Photo: Jim Frank.*

through Jansen's Paris headquarters, this mantel was originally intended for the second-floor Yellow Oval Room but was later deemed too small for it. The mantel's subsequent use in the Family Dining Room dictated the painting of the existing gray stone baseboards in imitation of dark-green marble.

Sister Parish had Albert Hadley design a series of proposals for the windows. The first was a translation of mid-eighteenth-century English patterns espoused by the likes of Thomas Chippendale and Robert Adam, with elaborately carved and gilded cornices. A second proposal incorporated American eagles on top of wood valances that were extensions of the room's cornice. Although beautiful in concept, these designs were not favored by Jacqueline Kennedy, who directed Parish and Hadley to a less elaborate version of the second proposal. The installed draperies consisted of plain panels of yellow silk that were double-tied with ornamental cording and tassels. They were installed within the architectural moldings of the windows, following Henry du Pont's direction.

For furniture and art, Parish and du Pont concentrated on the American Federal style. A period dining table with fluted pedestal legs was surrounded by the previously noted Sheraton-style chairs. To the right of the door to the State Dining Room, Jacqueline Kennedy and du Pont placed an elaborate breakfront made for the Willing family of Philadelphia in 1800. A mahogany sideboard with tambour central doors and cast pulls showing the likeness of George Washington was positioned along the west wall. Other additions included a New York gilt convex mirror, which was placed above the mantel, and an exceptional equestrian portrait of Brigadier General John Hartwell Cocke by artist Edward Troye, which was positioned between the windows.

For the floor, the First Lady intended to have the Engelhards purchase a period carpet. However, when the Troye portrait became available for purchase, Jane Engelhard asked Mrs. Kennedy which she would rather have. Jacqueline Kennedy selected the painting. In part, her choice was based on the wear that so many of the fine period rugs previously acquired for other White House rooms were already showing signs of; she was thus not certain that the purchase of another antique carpet, for a highly used dining room, no less, was a wise decision. Certainly her own love of horses further encouraged the selection of the portrait as the chosen gift. Thus, a contemporary carpet featuring

Family Dining Room, looking north, November 25, 1963, showing the table set for the reception following the funeral of President Kennedy. The installed drapery design was a simplification of the designs made for the room by Albert Hadley for Sister Parish. Courtesy John F. Kennedy Library.

pink roses on a gold lattice and off-white background was installed in the room in early 1963.

The redecorated Family Dining Room was really created for the President of the United States. John F. Kennedy used it for numerous congressional and business breakfasts during the week, and he seemed pleased with its reincarnation from a dark, somewhat dreary space to a bright and inviting room.

The First Lady was less complimentary of the transformation. Presumably this was dictated by Sister Parish's control of the Family Dining Room project. Indeed, the New York decorator's justifiable frustration with Stéphane Boudin's domination of other White House rooms made Parish resolved to keep the Frenchman from participating in the Family Dining Room effort. For Jacqueline Kennedy, this alienation of Boudin assured a lack of enthusiasm for the proposed scheme and helped to define the completed space as "her most un-favorite of all White House rooms."[5]

CHAPTER TWELVE

The Yellow Oval Room

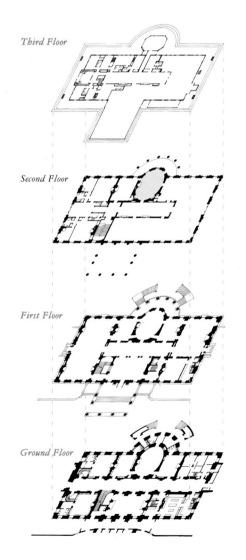

Third Floor

Second Floor

First Floor

Ground Floor

The creation of the Yellow Oval Room fulfilled the Kennedys' wish for a semiformal drawing room in the private quarters of the White House. Similar in shape to the more familiar Blue Room below, the second-floor Oval Room offered picturesque views of rolling lawns and the city's famous monuments beyond. Having served various functions throughout its history, the room had been used by recent presidents as a private study. For the Kennedys, the room first became a transplant of their Georgetown living room and, eventually, a more formal Louis XVI drawing room. Its decoration was inevitably credited to Sister Parish, who formulated the decoration of most of the family quarters. However, the finished room was, in reality, a compilation of the efforts of Parish, Jacqueline Kennedy, Jayne Wrightsman, and Stéphane Boudin.

Sister Parish developed the concept for the room during the weeks between the November election and the January Inauguration. Breaking away from the predominant blue-and-white color scheme of the bedrooms, Parish had the walls painted a soft yellow above the chair rail to the cornice line. The parquet wood floor was covered with a deeper yellow cut-pile carpet trimmed with an off-white fringe. On this the New York decorator arranged the off-white slipcovered chairs and sofas from the Kennedys' previous residence, along with comparable pieces taken from White House storage. A set of Louis XVI–style chairs from the Georgetown dining room was also used in the room. (These chairs no doubt reflected the First Lady's desire to furnish the room in "Louis XVI which Presidents Madison and Jefferson

PAGE 162: *President and Mrs. Kennedy in the completed Yellow Oval Room, March 20, 1963. In the background can be seen Stéphane Boudin's window treatment and a pedestal candelabrum. Courtesy John F. Kennedy Library.*

BELOW: *Collection of textiles and trimmings approved for the Yellow Oval Room. Courtesy Parish-Hadley, New York. Photo: Jim Frank.*

BELOW RIGHT: *Jacqueline Kennedy's personal study for the upholstery and furniture placement in the Yellow Oval Room, late 1961. Courtesy Parish-Hadley, New York. Photo: Jim Frank.*

both loved & had in the White House.")[1] Although far from complete, the room quickly became the President and First Lady's favorite for entertaining friends.

In June 1961 Parish arranged for the completion of the room's decoration to be financed by her friends John and Frances Loeb, both of whom were established connoisseurs of French Impressionist paintings. The Loebs had been made aware of the room's importance during a private dinner at the White House. Their gift covered the acquisition of furniture, the fabrication of draperies, and additional costs that arose in the process of making the room the centerpiece of the Kennedys' living quarters. Hearing of the gift while in Switzerland, Jayne Wrightsman was ecstatic. In her July 18 letter of congratulations to Parish, she noted, "You really are a wonder! Bravo!"[2]

Wrightsman continued her letter by adding another update—part of a series that she had been directing to both Parish and the First Lady—regarding possible Louis XVI antiques for the Yellow Oval Room. In this particular edition she made note of a chandelier with "estimates from Jansen for the work they would do."[3] This mention of Jansen must have taken away from the letter's congratulatory intent, for it no doubt reaffirmed Parish's growing concern about the Paris-based decorating firm's involvement with the White House. Indeed, references to Jansen or its president, Stéphane Boudin, had

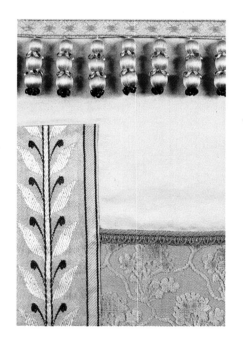

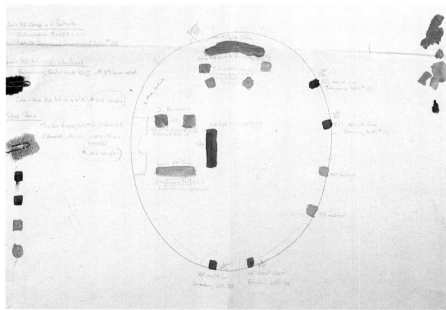

The completed Yellow Oval Room of the White House, ca. late-1962. Courtesy John F. Kennedy Library.

become common in both letters and conversations regarding various aspects of the restoration project, including a proposal for draperies for the Oval Room. Feeling pushed aside by Boudin, Parish threatened to resign from the Fine Arts Committee.

Wrightsman and the First Lady both sought to stop her from doing this. Acknowledging her importance with regard to providing donors as well as access to the decorating trade, Jacqueline Kennedy designated the Yellow Oval Room an exclusive project of the New York decorator in a most conciliatory letter written on June 30. The First Lady noted that even though she had wanted to utilize Boudin's drapery design for a number of months, she would bow to the wishes of the donors whose friendship with Parish seemingly made that impossible.[4]

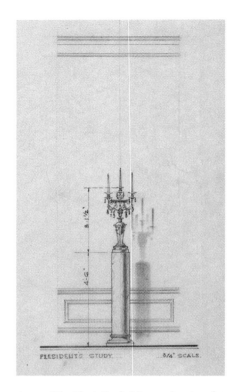

ABOVE: *"President's Study." Jansen drawing of proposed pair of marble columns for use with antique candelabra, late 1961. Courtesy Paul Manno. Photo: Jim Frank.*

ABOVE RIGHT: *Photostat of Stéphane Boudin's second proposal for the Yellow Oval Room window treatments. Sister Parish adapted this design to hang within the moldings, following the preference of Henry du Pont, although it was intended to be installed over the window moldings. Courtesy Parish-Hadley, New York. Photo: Jim Frank.*

However secure Sister Parish may have felt upon receiving the First Lady's letter, she was soon made aware of a continuing Boudin presence. Eighteen days after reassuring Parish of her independence with regard to the Yellow Oval Room, Jacqueline Kennedy attempted to sell the New York designer on the Paris-born window treatment. In a very upbeat letter, the First Lady informed Parish that Jayne Wrightsman had secured Boudin's personal permission to use his designs as her own.[5] Whether recognizing a losing battle or simply accepting the consolation that the room's overall decoration would be credited to her anyway, Parish used Boudin's design, which called for yellow taffeta panels falling straight to the floor from swag-like valances; the center window had a symmetrical valance while the left and right windows followed an asymmetrical design.

Sister Parish did declare independence of a sort with regard to how the draperies were to be installed. This became necessary if the room were to be completed on schedule, as Boudin was constantly revising his proposals. In early September 1961 the Frenchman forwarded to Jayne Wrightsman, who subsequently forwarded to the White House, two versions of an updated design for the windows. The first was a new concept showing the draperies installed over the moldings and the second an adaptation of the previously accepted proposal—probably based on a Henry du Pont dictum—installed within the frames. Wrightsman wrote the First Lady that both she and Boudin favored the former, which increased the exposure of the windows, important "particularly as you use the doors to go out on the porch."[6] Jacqueline Kennedy agreed and directed the change to Parish.

President Kennedy standing in front of the Yellow Oval Room mantelpiece on June 22, 1961. Placed in front of the mantel is a scale mock-up of the green and white mantelpiece brought to the attention of Mrs. Kennedy by Jayne Wrightsman and purchased for the Yellow Oval Room by Mr. and Mrs. John Loeb. After consideration, the mantel was deemed too small for the room and it was instead incorporated into the redecoration of the Family Dining Room on the State floor. Courtesy John F. Kennedy Library.

On September 16 Sister Parish responded with concern "as we have had so many changes [to the design of the draperies already]. . . . Mr. du Pont has approved of the original drawing to be hung inside the trim of the windows . . . [and] this complete new treatment presents a drastic problem as the changes would require yardages to be totally different."[7] The emphasis given to Mr. du Pont's approval was surely intended as a reminder that the Loeb gift was made to the Fine Arts Committee—which was chaired by du Pont—and not some independent group led by Boudin. The First Lady did not focus on this reference. Instead, she recognized the relevance of the previously ordered

President Kennedy meeting with foreign officials in the yet-to-be-completed Yellow Oval Room, October 5, 1961. Courtesy John F. Kennedy Library.

yardage having already been woven by Scalamandré; additional yardage might not have matched exactly. Perhaps remembering that last-minute changes to the design of tassel fringe and decorative tape for the same draperies required discarding some costly materials, the First Lady followed Parish's lead and abandoned efforts to implement further changes. The window treatment was Boudin's, but a compilation of the Frenchman's old and new proposals.

The furniture for the Oval Room was equally difficult to select. In June 1961 Jayne Wrightsman found a large suite of Louis XVI furniture in Paris that she described as follows: "Stamped J. B. Lelarge consisting of a canape, six arm chairs + six side chairs . . . the price is $15,000.00 for the set."[8] Wrightsman continued by noting that the suite "would be more simple than the gold chairs but I think it might be very chic + in some ways more practical."[9] Although she deemed the furniture ideal for the Oval Room, going so far as to guess how much Jansen would charge to repaint it ("between 2 + $3,000.00"), Wrightsman recognized that others might have to be convinced. Apparently the best way to do that was to make it seem that they were leading the way. "I think you have chosen well," she wrote to Sister Parish on July 18. "The more I think about it," she continued, "the more I think that gilt

The Yellow Oval Room looking toward the President's bedroom, 1962. Among the First Lady's personal items included in the decoration of the room were the large fur placed over the sofa and the assembled pair of consoles. On either side of the sofa are brass and mahogany tables supplied by Jansen. Courtesy John F. Kennedy Library.

furniture with the plain painted walls might be too pompous. . . . [T]he white furniture is really very charming, not too fragile and the sort of furniture that might have been ordered for the White House."[10]

Once purchased, the suite was scheduled to be placed in the center of the room, in line with the fireplace. Jacqueline Kennedy worked with Parish to plan the general placement as well as the upholstery. Regarding the selection of fabrics, the First Lady wanted variety: "I thought to have side chairs yellow too [along with the sofa and arm chairs] makes too many . . . a suite look which I hate. They could be green but I rather like brown—so lets [*sic*] try it—as its [*sic*] just for 4 side chairs + if its [*sic*] a mistake I'll redo it myself."[11] Whether this proposal was carried out is not known. Brown was introduced on one of two fully upholstered couches that were added to the room soon after the arrival of the painted suite. However, the darker color evidently didn't work with the overall scheme and the brown couch was soon recovered in yellow.

The final arrangement of the furniture was in place by early 1962. It was a combined effort between Sister Parish and Stéphane Boudin, although Parish was probably not aware of it. Indeed, Boudin's ideas were not directed to Parish but anonymously transmitted through the First Lady and Jayne

Wrightsman. The Lelarge painted furniture was upholstered in a yellow cut velvet, with a traditional French box treatment given to the seats and backs. The sofa and four armchairs from the suite were located not at the center of the room as originally intended but in front of the windows. Four of the side chairs were placed flanking two consoles on the room's west side. At the center, before the fireplace, were the two gold-taffeta-upholstered couches and—a most important feature—one of the President's famous rocking chairs. Nearby stood two writing tables, one framed by a pair of painted English armchairs that were first upholstered in Truman-era green silk, then orange velvet, and finally a Boudin-selected black and ivory striped silk via Paris.

Stéphane Boudin and Jansen soon dominated the selection process for the room's remaining furnishings. Boudin selected a pair of gilt bronze candelabra with crystal droplets, which were mounted on dark marble columns and placed between the windows. He also directed Wrightsman to a green and white marble mantelpiece with a large eagle in the center tablet. She quickly defended it when writing to Parish: "The mantel . . . for the oval room happens to come from Jansen. I recommended it—not because of Boudin but because it would be a dream for the White House."[12] (The mantel was purchased, but soon it was deemed too small for the room. It was later installed in the Family Dining Room, where it remains today.) Additional acquisitions

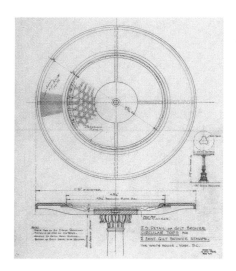

Jansen's proposal for two standing ashtrays incorporating plates from the Rutherford B. Hayes dinner service, May 12, 1962. Courtesy Paul Manno. Photo: Jim Frank.

were made, including a pair of painted bergères, two gueridons, two small Louis XVI worktables, two writing tables, and four bouillotte lamps.

The Kennedys added—and subtracted—a variety of personal possessions to the Loeb-donated furnishings during the formulation of the Yellow Oval Room. For a time the famous Louis XVI bureau plat that was included in Sotheby's 1996 auction of the former First Lady's possessions was prominently positioned in the room. Signed "E. Levasseur" and used by the President to sign the 1963 Nuclear Test Ban Treaty, the desk had been chosen as a permanent fixture for the Oval Room by Jansen. Jayne Wrightsman's husband, Charles, offered to pay for the piece if Jacqueline Kennedy wanted it for the White House. However, the First Lady's fondness for the writing desk led her to tell Jansen's Paul Manno that the bill should be directed not to Wrightsman but to the Kennedy family offices in New York.[13] Other Kennedy-owned furnishings included an Italian games table, two small needlepoint rugs, a "table vide poche," two brass-mounted consoles, Aubusson tapestry pillows, black lacquer coffee tables, and a pair of Paris porcelain vases mounted as lamps.

Eventually the White House acquired similar pieces to substitute for the Kennedy-owned furnishings. This became necessary when the President and First Lady began building their own house in the hills outside of Middleburg, Virginia. Jansen tracked down everything from "one pair of Empire urns, mounted as lamps" to "one Louis XVI mahogany commode with gilded bronze mounts."[14] The commode was intended to replace a console that stood to one side of the door leading to the President's bedroom. When efforts to find a similar piece for the opposite side of the door proved unsuccessful, Boudin proposed duplicating the existing piece. "We will make one reproduction of the large Louis XVI commode in the Yellow Drawing room," recorded a March 8, 1963, estimate. "It will be made of Honduras mahogany with gilded bronze mounts and a shaped marble top . . . Price . . . $1,895.00."[15] The reproduction was approved and in place by the middle of the year.

The First Lady also wanted coffee tables to exchange for her fragile lacquer ones. Boudin proposed a standard Jansen design—a gilded wood Louis XVI–style table with glass top. Recognizing the sensitivity of Sister Parish to anything associated with the Paris-based firm, the First Lady proposed the idea as her own. To an unsuspecting Parish, Jacqueline Kennedy suggested Louis XVI coffee tables. Her assessment was that white tables would be too fussy but that gold ones might be just right. The First Lady also noted that glass tops might afford a sense of lightness as well as an opportunity to appreciate the rugs below.[16]

Although Jacqueline Kennedy saw the Yellow Oval Room as somewhat of a personal domain, she recognized it as a room that could be appreciated by both men and women.[17] John F. Kennedy found the completed Louis XVI drawing room an inviting place for private meetings and gatherings of friends, and he referred to it as his "easy room."[18] The President's approval was further demonstrated by his participation in the design and installation of stereo speakers in the room's built-in bookcases as well as his concern for details such as the firmness of cushions for guests.

And for the First Lady, the room had no rival. "I never dreamt anything so perfect could happen," wrote Jacqueline Kennedy to John Loeb upon the room's completion. "A million, million thanks!"[19] The Yellow Oval Room was the most completely French room in the White House, and this alone made it one of the First Lady's favorites. More important, it was within this room that John F. Kennedy, the politician, and Jacqueline Kennedy, the publicity-shy wife, shared an appreciation for life in the White House. Indeed, more than any other space, the Yellow Oval Room best represented their ideal backdrop for the Presidency—inviting yet somewhat formal, inspired by history while fashionable and chic. With this in mind, it is not surprising that the Yellow Oval Room was Jacqueline Kennedy's choice for privately receiving France's President Charles de Gaulle, England's Prince Philip, and Ireland's President Eamon de Valera after her husband's funeral. For the Kennedys, the upstairs Oval Room was "the heart of the White House."[20]

CHAPTER THIRTEEN

Guest Rooms

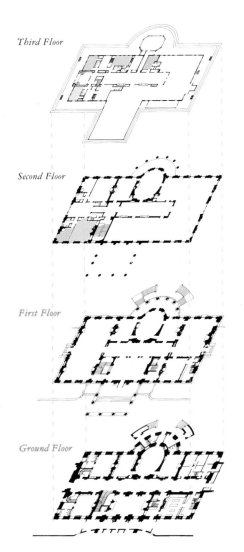

Third Floor

Second Floor

First Floor

Ground Floor

An aspect often overlooked when viewing the White House is that it is the personal residence of the incumbent First Family. Thus it is used not only for official events but also for private entertaining. For Jacqueline Kennedy, one of the more disconcerting aspects of living in the White House was the "hotel"-like quality of the guest rooms. In the less than three years that she lived in the mansion, she oversaw the redecoration of the majority of these rooms. Beyond changes to the decor, the First Lady directed the inclusion of fresh flowers and current magazines as well as new linens, "attractive" cigarette boxes, hampers, and even wicker wastebaskets. Her efforts were intended to relieve the mansion of what she herself had defined as an "Early Statler"[1] appearance.

THE QUEENS' BEDROOM

Also called the Rose Guest Room, the Queens' Bedroom is the feminine equivalent of the more famous Lincoln Bedroom on the other side of the second floor's East Sitting Hall. The room attained its royal name by serving five visiting European queens: Great Britain's Elizabeth, the current Queen Mother; her daughter, Queen Elizabeth II; the Netherlands' Wilhelmina and Juliana; and Greece's Frederika. While awaiting the completion of her own suite of rooms, Jacqueline Kennedy herself resided in the Queens' Room during her first weeks as First Lady.

Presumably it was because of her own familiarity with the Queens' Bedroom that the First Lady resisted furnishing the room completely with period antiques. Unlike the majority of other White House guest rooms, this room retained comfortable club chairs and a contemporary sofa and wing chair even after its final refurbishing in early 1963; the First Lady wanted guests to feel relaxed and less conscious of the museum-like atmosphere of other White House rooms. This was evidently to the frustration of Henry du Pont, who seems to have had other ideas for the room. In a November 29, 1962, letter to the First Lady, curator William Elder noted that "Mr. duPont [*sic*] came by for about an hour this morning and did a little furniture moving. He still wants to remove the comfortable sofa from the Queen's [*sic*] Room and replace it with an early nineteenth century one that we have not yet used."[2] Du Pont seems to have become further agitated by the following January, when he personally wrote to the curator that he hoped "regardless of the French desk and dressing table, I may see the Queen's [*sic*] Room more or less as it was planned; with the big sofa between the bed and the window and the small sofa down in the Library."[3] The Fine Arts Committee chairman's expressed frustration was no doubt due to the fact that Stéphane Boudin, the "proposer" of the French desk and dressing table, was in the process of formulating a completely separate plan for the bedroom.

Henry du Pont's discouragement led to an attempt to take matters regarding the Queens' Room's "proper" decoration into his own hands. In late 1962 du Pont independently accepted for the room a set of ca. 1824 French wallpaper by duFour entitled "Les Setes Grecques," which was to soon be

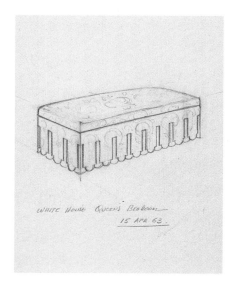

The completed Queens' Bedroom, looking north, July 31, 1963. Courtesy John F. Kennedy Library.

removed from the walls of the donor's house in Boston. He noted in a letter to the First Lady that the paper, consisting of scenes of ancient Greece, was "just right ... for the Queen's [*sic*] Room,"[4] and that, with her approval, he would arrange for Peter Guertler to hang it there as soon as possible. His letter prompted a long handwritten reply from Mrs. Kennedy expressing her disappointment that he had accepted the paper. She went on to explain that she had already arranged for the Queens' Room to be hung with rose-colored water silk she had shown him earlier. (Presumably "hung" refers to window and bed hangings, not the upholstery of the walls.) In the very considerate and

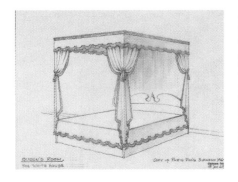

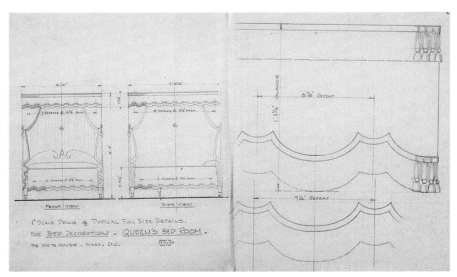

ABOVE: *"Queen's Room—The White House, Copy of Paris Dwg, 3 March 1962." Design submitted in June 1963 by Jansen's New York office proposing treatment for bed. Courtesy Paul Manno. Photo: Jim Frank.*

RIGHT: *"Bed Decoration—Queen's Bed Room." Jansen's design showing the four-poster bed with proposed hangings, January 23, 1963. Courtesy Paul Manno. Photo: Jim Frank.*

deferential tone that characterized all of the First Lady's letters to du Pont, she added that no more items should be accepted for the White House without checking with her, as the space available for new acquisitions such as wallpaper was running out.[5]

Jacqueline Kennedy's concern about the acceptance of the wallpaper had a great deal to do with the room's location in the mansion. As Rose Kennedy, the President's mother and occasional White House houseguest, later recalled, the Queens' Room "gets very little morning sun ... [and] the view from the windows is of Pennsylvania Avenue, a most noble name with many historic associations but ... [it is] visually rather drab."[6] The First Lady seems to have agreed with this assessment of the formal guest room, and she presumably directed Stéphane Boudin to keep the room light with walls and woodwork painted white. To further lighten the room, Boudin recommended —and Jacqueline Kennedy approved—the use of rather impractical off-white carpeting.

The Frenchman sent designs for the room's window draperies before he decided on an actual fabric. This is evident in a surviving drawing that shows two separate proposals for the windows of the Queens' Room rendered in blue and white gouache. The approved design, the one on the left, consisted of elaborate French headed drapery panels with fringe-trimmed swags, gigots, and tassels.

"Queens' Dressing R'm." Jansen's proposal for window treatment with scalloped valance, early 1963. Courtesy Paul Manno. Photo: Jim Frank.

Fulfilling the First Lady's desire to continue the rose, red, and white color scheme adopted earlier in the century, Boudin recommended the use of a printed rose and off-white silk taffeta for the room's two windows and existing early-nineteenth-century four-poster bed. For the Fine Arts Committee's assembled suite of New York Federal shield-back chairs, Boudin ordered a similarly colored rose and ivory silk brocade. Both of these textiles were made by Boudin's favored French textile manufacturer, Tassinari and Châtel. Per the First Lady's desire to keep the room light, Boudin directed the use of white silk damask for the reupholstery of the contemporary sofa and chairs as well as for a long bench at the end of the bed. Utilizing another trademark of his career, Boudin included a round table, draped in velvet, for in front of the fireplace. As a finishing touch, Jacqueline Kennedy ordered pink silk sheets ornamented with lilies of the valley along the hemmed edges.

Above the mantel Mrs. Kennedy placed an eighteenth-century gilt wood overmantel with a Dutch-inspired still life that had been presented to President Truman in 1951 by then–Princess Elizabeth of Great Britain. Elsewhere in the room she positioned Mrs. William Howard Taft's elegant 1910 portrait by Karl Kronstrand, which shows the White House in the background. Two small landscapes, one oil and the other watercolor, by American Impressionist Maurice Prendergast were displayed on either side of the bed, along with two mid-nineteenth-century oil-on-tin paintings of the U.S. Capitol.

THE QUEENS' SITTING ROOM

In the small dressing room off of the Queens' Bedroom, Boudin and the First Lady set about creating a more intimate sitting area. The end result was one of the most beautiful of the Kennedy-era interiors.

The White House assembled a collection of early- and mid-nineteenth-century black lacquer furniture for the Queens' Sitting Room. Along the room's west wall was positioned a stencil-decorated daybed, while in the center of the room stood a black lacquer table. A pair of black and gilt caned chairs, a papier-mâché table, and an elaborate eglomisé overmantel looking glass were also acquired for the room.

For the walls, draperies, daybed, and a pair of contemporary club chairs Boudin selected a heavy blue and white cotton fabric with a printed neoclas-

The Empire Guest Room. This was the first of the White House guest bedrooms to be completed. Walls, draperies, and upholstery utilized Scalamandré's early-nineteenth-century toile de jouy, "Homage à Franklin." Courtesy John F. Kennedy Library.

sical pattern of garlands, cherubs, and flowers. Presumably there was some doubt about using so much of this material in the corner room. However, after considering the option of using the fabric solely for the furniture upholstery and window hangings, the First Lady sent a large swatch back to the curator with a note approving its use for the walls as well.[7] In contrast to the fabric, the moldings and dado were painted white. An off-white carpet similar to that used in the Queens' Bedroom was complemented by white tambour curtains and a dressing table draped in the same fabric.

OTHER GUEST ROOMS

For the third-floor guest rooms concealed behind the White House roof's balustrade, the First Lady, Boudin, and du Pont directed the inclusion of new

Redecorated Empire Guest Room, looking toward the windows, May 1962. Courtesy John F. Kennedy Library.

acquisitions as well as numerous pieces of existing White House furniture. Rooms were named after decorative periods and motifs.

The Empire Guest Room was the first to be completed. As with the other rooms on the third floor, Boudin directed the removal of the existing picture molding as well as a more formal treatment for the doors to the hall and bathroom. The walls were upholstered in a red and white toile entitled "Hommage à Franklin," which was manufactured by Scalamandré of New York. (This fabric is more commonly known as "Apotheosis of Washington.") A sleigh bed on loan from the Smithsonian Institution was covered in the same fabric, as were two side chairs and a small settee. Against the wall the White House curator assembled a collection of nineteenth-century engravings honoring the life of George Washington.

The Pineapple Bedroom was a large double guest room that took its name from the pineapple finials on the acquired pair of mid-nineteenth-century beds. The walls of the bedroom and the accompanying sitting room were covered with a green Japanese silk wallpaper supplied by Jansen's New York office. Draperies and bedcovers were made of green and blue chintz, while the floor was covered with the Queens' Bedroom's old carpeting, which was specially dyed for the suite. For the sitting room or "Petit Salon," Jansen designed a banquette upholstered in strié velvet.

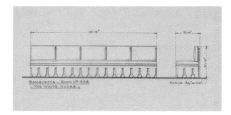

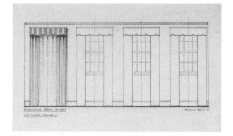

TOP: *"Banquette Room" (Pineapple Sitting Room). Design proposal submitted by Jansen in May 1963. Courtesy Paul Manno. Photo: Jim Frank.*
BOTTOM: *"Pineapple Room." Jansen's proposal for window treatments and alteration to architectural detail, raising the picture rail and eliminating the chair rail. Courtesy Paul Manno. Photo: Jim Frank.*
RIGHT: *Pineapple Bedroom, in the process of redecoration. Courtesy John F. Kennedy Library.*

The Country Bedroom manifested Henry du Pont's belief that each interior should have a specific decorative focus or period. This room represented the Federal period, ca. 1800–1810, with a simple tester bed trimmed with a hand-knotted lace canopy. On the bed was placed a mid-nineteenth-century appliqué quilt, while opposite the bed was hung a gilt Federal looking glass with acorn droplets. Much less elaborate than the Boudin-designed rooms, the Country Bedroom reflected the ideals of du Pont's own historic house museum, Winterthur.

Three other bedrooms followed similar methods of furnishing. Du Pont supplied a glazed floral chintz for "Room 303," which Boudin subsequently used for the covering of walls, window, and a French-style bed. Known as the "Orange Blossom" or "Chintz Bedroom," this interior was one which Boudin directed the removal of the existing chairrail and the raising of the picture molding.

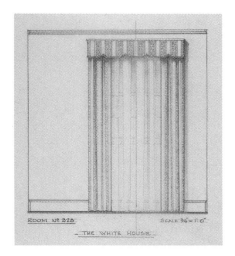

ABOVE: *Pineapple Sitting Room. Jansen's proposal for window treatment, May 1963. Courtesy Paul Manno. Photo: Jim Frank.*

RIGHT: *Chintz Bedroom on the third floor of the White House, after complete redecoration by Jansen, September 4, 1963. Courtesy John F. Kennedy Library.*

Another guest room was named for the blue toile used to drape the Chippendale-style four-post bed, which had been used in the Queens' Room during the Truman administration. For this room, Jacqueline Kennedy demonstrated frugalness by having President Grant's ca.1870 heart-shaped dining chairs camouflaged with slipcovers to allow them to blend with the late-eighteenth-century aspect of the overall decor.

Nearing completion at the time of the President's assassination, the guest rooms of the White House were given individual identities by the First Lady. Together, they served as extensions of the Kennedy style in entertaining.

CHAPTER FOURTEEN

The Victorian Taste

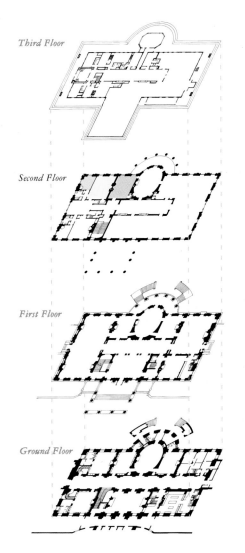

Third Floor

Second Floor

First Floor

Ground Floor

Although Jacqueline Kennedy personally abhorred everything Victorian, she sponsored the creation of two additional rooms representative of the melange of styles that developed during the second half of the nineteenth century. The First Lady also added pieces to the existing Lincoln Bedroom, which she described as nearly perfect after moving to the White House: "Can't change it—wouldn't want to."[1] This acknowledgment of decorative arts of a later period than that highlighted on the State and ground floors emphasized the restoration's goal of showcasing the entire history of the mansion. As Jacqueline Kennedy's third appointed Curator, James Ketchum, remembered: "During the first few months of the restoration, our goal may have been to reproduce the Monroe White House. Soon it became clear that this was impossible . . . the White House had to embrace all the major periods"[2] and the contributions of succeeding occupants.

THE LINCOLN BEDROOM

Although an admirer of the existing Lincoln Bedroom, the First Lady acknowledged that it could be improved upon. Eventually she and the White House curator included a pair of slipper chairs documented to the Lincoln administration; one of these was found by Mrs. Kennedy in a government warehouse, while its mate was returned to the White House by a Mrs. Millard Black of Arlington, Virginia. Upholstered in a late-nineteenth-century English William Morris–designed velvet donated by a Mrs. Burton Cohen of

PAGE 184: *The Restored Treaty Room, early 1963. The chandelier was originally one of three purchased for the White House by President Grant and later installed in the U.S. Capitol. This one was returned to the White House for Mrs. Kennedy's restoration through the efforts of Vice President Lyndon Johnson. Courtesy White House.*

BELOW: *The Lincoln Bedroom, 1963. Although not completely redecorated by Jacqueline Kennedy, this historic room received additions such as the pair of Morris velvet-upholstered slipper chairs and the English Regency brass chandelier. Courtesy John F. Kennedy Library.*

New Jersey, the chairs were later enhanced by an elaborate yellow and green twist fringe chosen by Stéphane Boudin. Curator William Elder proposed the inclusion of two tables from a suite of three ordered for the East Room by Andrew Jackson in 1829. "They are late Empire or Early Victorian in feeling," he noted in a memorandum to the First Lady, "and would be entirely appropriate."[3] Made by the famous nineteenth-century Philadelphia cabinetmaker Anthony Quervelle, these large marble-topped tables proved an appropriate scale for use on either side of the great Lincoln bed.

One of the final Kennedy additions to the Lincoln Bedroom was a chandelier. Throughout most of 1962 the First Lady repeatedly asked Jansen and the curator's office for suggestions for a ceiling-mounted fixture for the famous bedroom. By February 1963 Jansen's New York office had shipped a Regency brass fixture with hurricane shades. Not quite the Victorian gasolier with globes and prisms originally requested by the First Lady, this chandelier

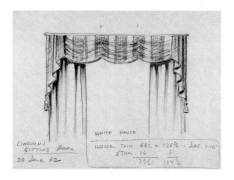

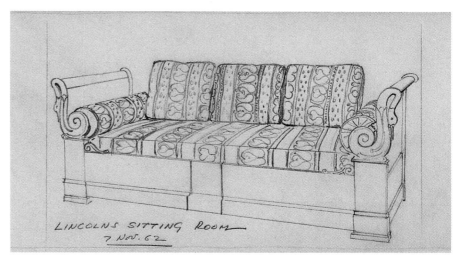

LINCOLNS SITTING ROOM
7 NOV. 62

ABOVE: *The original Jansen proposal for window valances in the Lincoln Sitting Room, June 29, 1962. Courtesy Paul Manno. Photo: Jim Frank.*
RIGHT: *"Lincoln's Sitting Room." Jansen proposal for swan-ornamented daybed, November 7, 1962. Courtesy Paul Manno. Photo: Jim Frank.*

was approved all the same. "Have the large brass ceiling fixture cleaned and electrified," recorded Paul Manno's February 1, 1963, notes on the White House project. It was installed by mid-1963, positioned in a modern, circular air vent at the center of the ceiling.

THE LINCOLN SITTING ROOM

In the small corner room adjoining the Lincoln Bedroom, Jacqueline Kennedy created another Victorian interior with the help of Jansen and the mansion's curators. Instantly called the Lincoln Sitting Room, this space had a more intimate scale due to a reduced ceiling height and overall size. From White House storage came four chairs—three side, one arm—believed to have been ordered for the mansion by Mary Todd Lincoln. For the chairs' upholstery, Jansen and the First Lady selected a red pressed velvet produced by Brunschwig and Fils of New York. A later-nineteenth-century tufted chair, also retrieved from a government warehouse, was covered in gold silk damask and similarly colored nine-inch fringe. Positioned along the east wall was a ca. 1830 mahogany daybed with swan-shaped arms. For this piece Boudin designed a cover with accompanying bolsters made from a French paisley-patterned cotton fabric.

For the walls and windows, Jansen continued the use of French printed cottons. The walls were upholstered with an olive-green and yellow fabric that Jansen's Paul Manno personally brought over from France. For the windows, Stéphane Boudin submitted a series of proposals for a valance treatment,

including a traditional swag effect utilizing the same paisley as that used for the daybed. However, the accepted proposal featured solid, straight valances of the same fabric used on the walls, with an applied horizontal band of paisley. The straight-falling curtain panels were made from a similar combination of the two printed textiles.

Finding a chandelier for the Lincoln Sitting Room demonstrated Jacqueline Kennedy's efforts to get the most for the money spent. Jansen submitted a "black and gold chandelier, price $970.00" for the room, which was "accepted in principle"[4] as of February 1963. Although pleased with Jansen's chandelier, the First Lady felt that the asking price was too high. Thus, while Jansen waited for final approval of the sale, the mansion's curator went to New York to see if he could find something less costly. "At a dealer on Second Avenue," described William Elder to Jacqueline Kennedy, "I found a small green and gold tole chandelier, French Empire about 1830–40. It is entirely original and has never been wired, etc. . . . I have asked Jimmy Biddle [of The Metropolitan Museum of Art] to take a look at it to double check. It is $350.00 and I thought most appropriate for the Lincoln Sitting Room."[5] Saving $620.00 for the restoration, the First Lady returned the Jansen chandelier and had the curator install his new find in the small sitting room.

Other finishing touches were selected and arranged by the First Lady. Civil War–era prints and memorabilia about the sixteenth President were framed and placed on the walls. Among the selected images was a color lithograph of Lincoln and his family published by Thomas Kelly of New York, and a Lincoln Inauguration Ball program with original satin ribbon tie. A ca. 1884 plaster cast of John Rogers's *Neighboring Pews*—a sculpture grouping of four individuals attending church services—was stationed in the far corner opposite the room's only door. Jacqueline Kennedy utilized a painted metal tray supported by a brass stand as a coffee table; this was later replaced with a more substantial mahogany butler's tray and base from the existing stock of White House furniture. For the decoration of these tables, the First Lady selected soup plates from the Rutherford B. Hayes china—the most elaborate Presidential dining service ever commissioned. Each of the Haviland-manufactured pieces displayed a different example of native flora or fauna as its central overglaze design. More than just decorative, these plates were given new roles as ashtrays.

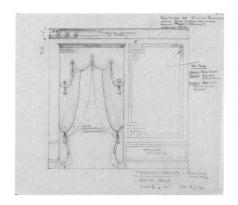

ABOVE: *"Lincoln's Cabinet" (Treaty Room). Jansen's proposal for installation of wallpaper borders and window draperies submitted in November 1961. When planning the redecoration of the Treaty Room, Stéphane Boudin contemplated using two gilt wood cornices from the White House collection. When the approved design was fabricated and ready for installation, the cornices could not be found. A substitution of additional velvet was made for the finishing of the drapery tops. Courtesy Paul Manno. Photo: Jim Frank.*

ABOVE RIGHT: *The Treaty Room prior to its redecoration, late 1961. Courtesy John F. Kennedy Library.*

THE TREATY ROOM

The greatest expression of Victoriana came with the creation of the Treaty Room. In what formerly had been the Monroe Room—Mrs. Herbert Hoover's tribute to the fifth President—Jacqueline Kennedy sponsored the formulation of a second-floor reception space that could double as a late-night conference room for the President. The double-windowed chamber had served as the cabinet room from 1865 to 1902, when the offices and private quarters of presidents shared the same floor. Indeed, the room's name was inspired by the many important documents negotiated and signed within its walls.

This most dramatic of the three White House interiors devoted to later-nineteenth-century American taste and fashion was one of Frenchman Stéphane Boudin's greatest successes. He utilized the mansion's vast quantity of nineteenth-century Gothic, Rococo, and Renaissance Revival furniture, much of which was retrieved from government warehouses. Boudin directed the placement of the Grant-era cabinet table, dining chairs, and large sofa, as well as monumental works of art such as Théobald Chartran's *Signing of the Peace Protocol Between Spain and the United States, August 12, 1898,* which measures nearly five feet by seven feet. To this eclectic melange of objects the First Lady added specially commissioned reproductions of famous treaties dating from the time when the room served as the executive branch of government's control center.

Stéphane Boudin photographed by Jacqueline Kennedy in the Treaty Room prior to its redecoration, late 1961. Courtesy John F. Kennedy Library.

The walls of the new Treaty Room were covered with deep-green flocked paper. For placement against the velvet-like surface Boudin designed geometric borders based on a decorative treatment chosen for the State Rooms during the administration of Andrew Johnson. The red diamond-patterned paper used to make these panels was copied from the wallpaper in the room across from Ford's Theater in which Johnson's predecessor, Abraham Lincoln, died. This treatment of walls was far from the soft palettes adopted by other American historic houses interpreting the same period. Boudin's dark-green and red geometric scheme was really the first twentieth-century attempt of significance to duplicate the strong contrasts of color, texture, and form that together had been popular immediately after the Civil War.

ABOVE: *Ca. 1880 stereopticon view of the Red Room of the White House. The framed panels that inspired Stéphane Boudin's treatment of the Treaty Room walls are visible in this post–Civil War image. Authors' collection.*

FACING PAGE: *President Kennedy signing the Nuclear Test Ban Treaty in the restored Treaty Room of the White House on October 7, 1963. Courtesy John F. Kennedy Library.*

For the windows Boudin devised somewhat elaborate draperies of wine-colored velvet with lace under-curtains. The velvet valances were designed for installation beneath a pair of late-nineteenth-century gilt cornices from the White House's collection. Whether misplaced or deemed inappropriate for the completed scheme, the intended cornices were not part of the finished window treatments. Additional velvet and trimmings were added to the tops of the already fabricated valances to hide this last-minute change.

In the process of restoration at the time of her televised tour of the White House, the Treaty Room was described by Jacqueline Kennedy as "a chamber of horrors."[6] However, she added that "when this room is finished you'll see how impressive it will be."[7] Certainly one of the features that made it truly impressive was an enormous three-tier chandelier. Originally purchased as one of a set of three for President Grant's 1873 redecoration of the East Room, the crystal and bronze fixture had been removed from the White House during the 1902 renovation and subsequently relocated to the U.S. Capitol. Vice President Lyndon Johnson and the Senate majority and minority leaders joined to return the chandelier from the Senate Connecting Corridor, and it was installed shortly after the completion of the other decorative changes to the room.

LEFT: *Jacqueline Kennedy formally receiving the chandelier returned from the U.S. Capitol, 1962. Courtesy John F. Kennedy Library.*

When completed, the Treaty Room was the epitome of a room designed as a backdrop for historic events. This was acknowledged when President Kennedy selected it for the signing of the 1963 Nuclear Test Ban Treaty, the document that represented the first sign of a thaw in the Cold War and, thus, one of the Kennedy administration's greatest achievements.

CHAPTER FIFTEEN

The Private Rooms

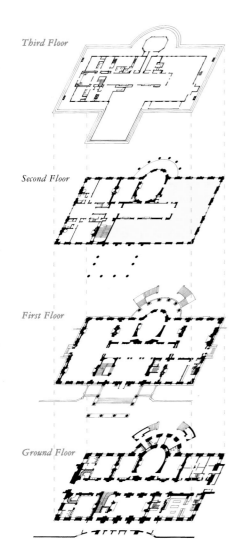

Third Floor

Second Floor

First Floor

Ground Floor

For John and Jacqueline Kennedy, the private quarters of the White House began as direct translations of rooms from their Georgetown house. However, as they became accustomed to calling the White House home, the decor of their private rooms became much more distinct and individual. Sister Parish served as the primary decorator for the President's bedroom, the First Lady's bedroom and dressing room, and the bedrooms of John and Caroline. However, by mid-1961 Stéphane Boudin began to expand his influence on the redecoration of the White House, moving from the State and ground floors to the family quarters. At the close of the Kennedy administration, the Frenchman was well ensconced in a complete reassessment of the Parish-designed rooms.

For the President there existed another private space in the West Wing of the White House. The indoor swimming pool, which had originally been built for Franklin Roosevelt in the 1930s, became the one place John F. Kennedy could relax with his children without straining his injured back. In recognition of this, the President's father, Ambassador Joseph P. Kennedy, commissioned the artist Bernard LaMotte to personalize the somewhat institutional facility with a painted mural of a Carribean scene.

THE PRESIDENT'S BEDROOM

For the President's room, Sister Parish and the First Lady removed the Grand Rapids furnishings selected during the Truman renovation, replacing them with an array of period antiques and contemporary upholstered pieces. A new

PAGE 196: *The President's bedroom, looking toward the fireplace, as decorated by Sister Parish, May 1963. Courtesy John F. Kennedy Library.*

BELOW: *The President's bedroom, looking toward the South Wall and windows. The first major piece of fine furniture donated to the White House during the Kennedy restoration, an eighteenth-century Philadelphia tall chest, can be seen at center. Above the chest is one of two Childe Hassam Flag Day paintings displayed in the President's bedroom. Courtesy John F. Kennedy Library.*

color scheme of blue and white was adopted for the room, which was situated next to the upstairs Oval Room. Against walls and carpeting of off-white, Parish placed a four-poster bed, which she covered in a blue and white cotton toile with a pattern of angels, garlands, and flowers. Originally proposed for Caroline Kennedy's bedroom, the fabric had been greatly admired by the President, who revealed to Parish that "I've always loved angels."[1] For the slipcovering of a pair of club chairs positioned before the fireplace, Parish selected an open-weave blue and white fabric. For the President's rocking chair and an accompanying wing chair, she used an off-white sailcloth. The overall effect was informal and comfortable.

Among the significant objects included in the President's bedroom was the first piece of American furniture donated to the Kennedy White House—

The First Lady's bedroom as designed by Sister Parish, 1961. Although originally intending pale green walls and white woodwork, Jacqueline Kennedy quickly changed her mind and requested the same off-white walls used in the President's bedroom. Courtesy John F. Kennedy Library.

an eighteenth-century Chippendale-style highchest. In early 1963 *Flag Day,* a patriotic painting by American Impressionist Childe Hassam, was given to the White House and hung on the room's north wall. A second Hassam canvas, presumably on loan, was placed above the highchest. Flanking the mantel was a pair of early-nineteenth-century English equestrian portraits owned by the President and First Lady.

Except for the removal of President Kennedy's personal possessions, the decoration of this bedroom did not change when Lyndon Johnson assumed the Presidency.

THE FIRST LADY'S BEDROOM AND DRESSING ROOM

In recalling life in the White House, Jacqueline Kennedy noted that "I wanted our bedroom to be the same as it was in Georgetown. I had my same curtains copied for there. They had been rather country-type material, and, of course, they looked absurd as the proportions of the room were so formal."[2] Parish worked with the First Lady on transferring the general feel of the Georgetown room to the much larger scale of 1600 Pennsylvania Avenue. Although the room was used by both Kennedys, Sister Parish placed a greater emphasis on its serving as the personal domain of the First Lady.

The First Lady's bedroom in the process of being redesigned by Stéphane Boudin, who reconfigured the furniture arrangement and included one of the President's own rocking chairs. At the time of the assassination of President Kennedy, Boudin was designing new draperies for the windows as well as a more architectural headboard for the bed. Courtesy John F. Kennedy Library.

The walls and carpeting of the room were of the same off-white as that used in the President's Bedroom. To this Parish added accents of blue, water green, and ivory. The draperies were made of a simple cotton fabric with white and green daisies on a water-green field. A Lawson-style loveseat was covered in a white quilted fabric, while Louis XV and Louis XVI–style chairs were upholstered in white damask, green silk, and a gold-on-ivory cut velvet. A silk-draped table was placed to one side of the white marble mantelpiece, atop which were arranged photographs of the President and the children. On the mantel, as throughout the room, Parish and the First Lady placed pieces of blue and white Chinese porcelain.

The bed was made up of two side-by-side mattresses, one consisting of the firm horsehair required for the President's back condition. The upholstered headboard was crowned by a water-green silk canopy. At the foot of the bed sat a long bench on which Jacqueline Kennedy placed current books as well as articles and files relating to the restoration project.

The First Lady's bed as designed by Sister Parish and Jacqueline Kennedy. The door at the right leads into the First Lady's dressing room. Courtesy John F. Kennedy Library.

The art for the room reflected Mrs. Kennedy's fondness for eighteenth- and nineteenth-century drawings and sculpture. On the mantel sat an eighteenth-century French terra-cotta bust of a child, a prized possession that the First Lady later had included in her official White House portrait. Above the bust, Jacqueline Kennedy and Sister Parish arranged three rows of eighteenth- and nineteenth-century drawings. A central position was given to a 1775 watercolor of a snow owl by English artist Peter Paillon. Other drawings and studies of animals were displayed elsewhere in the room, reflecting Jacqueline Kennedy's passion for wildlife.

By 1962 Stéphane Boudin began to plan a reinterpretation of the First Lady's bedroom. Surely it was he who convinced Jacqueline Kennedy that the draperies made by Parish were of too simple a fabric for the proportions and importance of the White House. In fall 1963 the Frenchman's influence on the First Lady was revealed when the Chief Usher of the White House was asked to hurry the fabrication of the new treatments along.[3] Presumably

The First Lady's dressing room, looking toward the windows, showing installation of Jansen's drapery design and wall coverings. Courtesy John F. Kennedy Library.

these never-completed draperies were to be made of a fine silk with elaborate trimmings.

For the bed, Boudin proposed replacing Parish's upholstered headboard with a Louis XVI–style example of painted wood. A photograph of a stock headboard was forwarded to the White House by Jansen. However, a decision had not been formulated by the time of the President's assassination in November 1963.

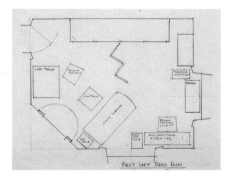

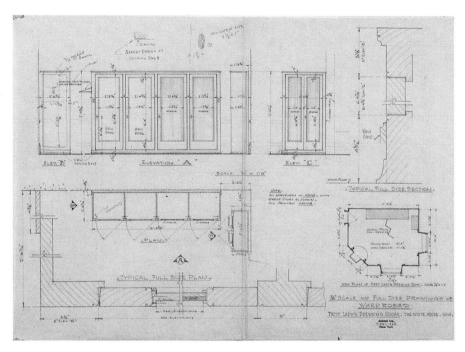

ABOVE: *"First Lady's Dress Room." Floorplan and furniture arrangement proposed by Jansen for boudoir. Courtesy Paul Manno. Photo: Jim Frank.*

RIGHT: *Elevations for the First Lady's boudoir, September 17, 1962. Jansen's plans for the wardrobe at top left indicate the placement of the trompe l'oeil doors. Courtesy Paul Manno. Photo: Jim Frank.*

While in the process of designing the new window treatments and headboard, Boudin assisted the First Lady in rearranging the room's furniture. This was done, presumably, to accommodate the inclusion of a writing table and chair for her use. The draped round table was removed from the grouping in front of the fireplace and the small loveseat relocated so that it backed up against the writing table. Suggesting a greater use of the room on the part of the President, one of his famous rocking chairs was introduced to this main seating area. The result was less feminine and more in keeping with expectations for a family living room than was the Parish-designed lady's boudoir.

Changes to the bedroom reflected an evolution of Jacqueline Kennedy's personal aesthetic. Stepping away from Sister Parish's design for the room, which was less than two years old, represented a growth indicative of Mrs. Kennedy's access to a broader spectrum of taste, knowledge, and luxury. Certainly one can see the influence of Stéphane Boudin in the refinement of her personal collection of furniture. From the nineteenth-century Dutch commode selected for placement between the room's windows to a Paris–to–New York search for a higher-quality pier looking glass, this room was in the process of becoming another example of Boudin's worldly style—familiar to the likes of Jayne Wrightsman, C. Z. Guest, and the Duchess of Windsor.

ABOVE: *Jansen artists' rendering for trompe l'oeil wardrobe. Courtesy Paul Manno. Photo: Jim Frank.*

RIGHT: *The First Lady's dressing room, looking toward the trompe l'oeil wardrobe. The open door leads into the First Lady's bedroom. Courtesy John F. Kennedy Library.*

Of course, the true expression of Boudin's style was the decoration of the adjoining dressing room. From this small corner room the Frenchman removed all traces of Parish's casual Southhampton vocabulary, replacing them with Paris-born silk and trompe l'oeil sophistication. The color scheme was blue and white, with the walls covered in a fine sky-colored paper-backed silk. For the windows Boudin designed elaborate draperies trimmed in tassel fringe. To complement the Frenchness of the room, Jansen created a white Louis XVI-style wood mantel for the existing corner fireplace.

Perhaps the most famous addition to the room was the trompe l'oeil painting of the doors to the First Lady's built-in wardrobe. Although consisting of four evenly spaced doors, the wardrobe was visually divided in two by Jansen. The two doors nearest the entrance to the room were painted by Paris-based artist Pierre-Marie Rudelle—"Artiste Peintre Décorateur"—to represent important events in the life of the First Lady. Among the images duplicated by the artist was a ca. 1935 photograph of a young Jacqueline Bouvier

"Dressing Table Mirror." Versions 1 and 2 of Jansen's proposed design for the First Lady's dressing table to be included in her boudoir, June 13, 1963. Courtesy Paul Manno. Photo: Jim Frank.

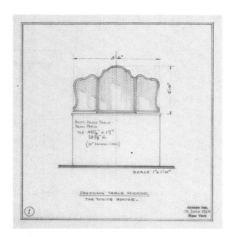 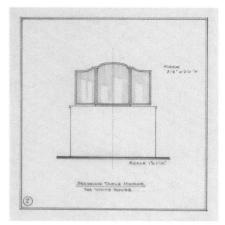

with her father after she placed in a Long Island horse show. Other images included John F. Kennedy's Pulitzer-winning *Profiles in Courage* and a *Look* magazine article showing the First Lady taking a spill during a Virginia fox hunt. The two remaining doors of the wardrobe had mirrored glass inserts and were hidden behind a four-panel French-painted screen displaying a Chinese water garden and faux-marble wainscoting. For the top of the wardrobe Rudelle produced five trompe l'oeil finials representing Dutch Baroque floral bouquets.

For the main seating area Boudin devised an elaborately tufted récamier on which the First Lady placed a leopard skin. Across from this stood one of a pair of French Provençal–style armchairs, which had loose blue silk seat and back cushions. For the nearby walls the First Lady and Boudin selected a series of plates from early-nineteenth-century French pattern books. The majority of these engravings illustrated designs for window treatments, and they no doubt reflected the grandeur that Boudin and Jacqueline Kennedy were introducing to the White House. Elsewhere the First Lady displayed an early-nineteenth-century hand-colored engraving of the French Empress Josephine.

Jacqueline Kennedy's concern for design and decoration was not above a need for the practical. For her dressing table she asked Jansen for a functional mirror. Jansen soon submitted five individual proposals, all of which consisted of a central piece of mirrored glass with two adjustable side panels. With its location from the two mirrored wardrobe doors, the First Lady was assured full review of her appearance while seated.

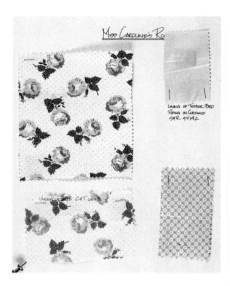

ABOVE: *Fabrics selected for "Miss Caroline's Room" by Sister Parish. Courtesy Parish-Hadley, New York. Photo: Jim Frank.*

RIGHT: *Caroline Kennedy's bedroom as decorated by Sister Parish, May 1962. Courtesy John F. Kennedy Library.*

THE CHILDREN'S ROOMS

Sister Parish had originally planned to have John and Caroline Kennedy placed across the West Sitting Hall from their mother's suite of rooms. However, with the introduction of a private dining room and kitchen on the family floor, the children's rooms were relocated to a series of rooms overlooking the north entrance to the mansion. Parish relied on Jacqueline Kennedy's wish to make these rooms not extensions of the White House but comfortable and lively spaces.

For "Miss Caroline's" bedroom, Parish again utilized off-white carpeting and walls. At the room's single window she placed rosebud-patterned chintz curtains and a valance with organdy undercurtains of the same pattern. In front of the fireplace, the Lawson-style loveseat and matching club chair were slipcovered in a small red-on-white lattice-patterned chintz. This provided the ideal background for Caroline's large menagerie of stuffed animals and dolls. The small canopy bed was draped in the same fabric as that used at the window. On the walls Jacqueline Kennedy personally arranged a variety of twentieth-century works of art, the most famous of which was Grandma Moses' *Fourth of July* from the White House collection.

John F. Kennedy, Jr.'s nursery as designed by Sister Parish, May 1962. Courtesy John F. Kennedy Library.

For brother John's room, the New York decorator selected a blue, pink, and white chintz for the curtains and slipcovers. As in Caroline's room, all of the furniture was painted white, with the exception of a miniature version of his father's famous rocking chair. A collection of toy soldiers was neatly arranged on the shelves of a built-in bookcase, while numerous planes, tanks, and trucks filled the storage cabinets below.

By early 1963 Jacqueline Kennedy was already thinking about the redecoration of the children's rooms for when she and her family would be gone from the White House. She wrote to Jansen's Paul Manno to ask that he remind Boudin about possible schemes for these rooms. The First Lady noted that they would probably be furnished with English-style pieces and

The White House swimming pool prior to the installation of the painted mural given by Ambassador Joseph P. Kennedy. Courtesy John F. Kennedy Library.

that perhaps one could be designed around the mansion's growing collection of blue and white Chinese Export porcelain. Somewhat premature, this inquiry all the same represented Jacqueline Kennedy's dedication to the restoration project. Her reasoning reflected a belief that not all of her successors would be as committed as she was to the appropriate furnishing of the mansion's rooms.

THE PRESIDENT'S POOL

If the First Lady's dressing room was the definitive expression of her tastes and interests, the enhancement of the existing White House swimming pool served

The White House swimming pool during the painting of the mural given by Ambassador Kennedy, showing artist Bernard LaMotte at work. Courtesy John F. Kennedy Library.

The White House swimming pool during the painting of the mural given by Ambassador Kennedy, showing artist Bernard LaMotte at work. Courtesy John F. Kennedy Library.

to reflect similar characteristics for the President. Soon after the Inauguration, the President's father commissioned artist Bernard LaMotte to paint a Caribbean bay scene with sailboats and docks for three sides of the pool; the fourth wall was covered in mirrored glass. This commissioned gift provided a relaxing environment for John F. Kennedy, who swam twice daily. The brightly colored mural defined the pool as the President's personal domain.

The personal spaces of the President and First Lady were not ceremonial but intimate reflections of their individual lifestyles. From the First Lady's dressing room, with its collection of period pattern book plates, to the swimming pool, with its surround of crystal blue waters of the Caribbean, John and Jacqueline Kennedy created a personally comforting environment behind the official backdrop of Camelot. "Beyond all the familiar tokens," fashion editor Diana Vreeland wrote, describing another aspect of the Kennedy White House, "there is a secret world."[4] No doubt the private quarters of the Kennedy White House formed just such a refuge.

The President's Office and Cabinet Room

West Wing

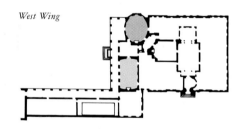

The decoration of the Oval Office conveys the taste, character, and ideology of the individual who works there. This is not by coincidence. Surely this room is one of the most photographed interiors in the United States, let alone the world. It is used daily as a backdrop for the signing of bills, the greeting of foreign dignitaries, and the presentation of citations and awards. It thus affords an opportunity to express whatever imagery is desired by a President. The Cabinet Room serves a similar role as a symbol of the executive branch of government in action. It is within this room that national policies are formulated and foreign and domestic crises are dealt with. Both utilitarian and symbolic, these rooms were recognized by the President and First Lady as unique formats for conveying the Kennedy administration's sense of style.

THE OVAL OFFICE

The Oval Office, originally designed for William Howard Taft in 1909, went through two redecorations during the Kennedy administration. The first was completed by Sister Parish and the First Lady in early 1961, and its intent was no doubt to represent the idealism, vigor, and youth of the President's proclaimed New Frontier. The elliptical walls were painted off-white; the Truman-era green carpet and draperies were retained. Parish divided the room into two distinct areas, the first a working station and the second a seating area. The centerpiece of the former was a carved oak desk presented to President Rutherford Hayes by Queen Victoria in 1880. Found on the ground

PAGE 210: *The Oval Office, looking toward the windows, August 1961. In this view stands the famous "Resolute" desk given by Queen Victoria to President Rutherford Hayes and rediscovered by Jacqueline Kennedy in the ground-floor broadcast room. Courtesy John F. Kennedy Library.*

floor of the mansion by Jacqueline Kennedy, the desk retained the original presentation plaque explaining its rich history.

> H.M.S. "RESOLUTE" forming part of the expedition sent in search of SIR JOHN FRANKLIN in 1852, was abandoned in latitude 74° 41' N. Longitude 101° 22' W. on 15th May 1854. She was discovered and extricated in September 1855, in latitude 67°N. By Captain Buddington of the United States whaler "George Henry." The ship was purchased, fitted out and sent to England, as a gift to her Majesty Queen Victoria by the President and the People of the United States, as a token of goodwill & friendship. This table was made from her timbers when she was broken up, and is presented by the QUEEN of GREAT BRITAIN & IRELAND TO THE PRESIDENT OF THE UNITED STATES, as a memorial of the courtesy and loving Kindness which dictated the offer of the gift of the "RESOLUTE."

For the seating area before the fireplace, Parish and the First Lady positioned two sofas and a coffee table formerly used by the Eisenhowers in the mansion's West Sitting Hall. Parish had the sofas slipcovered in an oatmeal-colored fabric from which she also had cushions made for the President's rocking chair. For above the fireplace, Jacqueline Kennedy borrowed from the Corcoran Gallery of Art Dominic Serres's War of 1812 seascape depicting the American ship *Bonhomme Richard* at battle with England's *Serapis.* Other nautical paintings, as well as models of ships from the President's personal collection, created a casual, youthful backdrop for the Kennedy presidency.

However, by mid-1962 plans began for a new scheme for the Oval Office. This one was to be more sophisticated in its design, perhaps suggesting a greater worldliness for the Kennedy Presidency. Stéphane Boudin worked with both the President and the First Lady on the formulation of this scheme, which was still incomplete at the time of the assassination on November 22, 1963.

It would be easy to assume that this second redecoration of the Oval Office was just the concern of Jacqueline Kennedy. However, the President was equally enthusiastic about the project. In an early memorandum to the mansion's chief usher, the First Lady revealed how much the President was involved with the room's redesign: "We don't want white chairs—he wants to see sample of rug—He says curtains are OK but I think perhaps they should be a creamier color—as it makes everything else in room look so dirty. . . ."[1]

The Oval Office, looking toward the fireplace, August 1961, as decorated by Sister Parish. The New York socialite-turned-decorator utilized the green draperies and carpet that were installed in 1947 and created a nautical theme using loaned seascapes as well as ship models from the President's personal collection. Courtesy John F. Kennedy Library.

In the end, the President's choice for a purer white for the draperies won out. In February 1963 Jansen's New York office recorded that "S. B. [Stéphane Boudin] To make the drapes without valance using a large rep white material with a large red and white border on the edge. . . . The curtains will be hung on rods which will be steel with gilded pineapple ends and rings."[2] Jansen also recorded that the draperies were "To come from Paris," a fact that is somewhat surprising, considering John F. Kennedy's well-known political concern about his wife's preference for almost everything French.

Proposal for window treatment in the Oval Office, dated November 23, 1962, from Jansen's Paris office. Stéphane Boudin formulated a number of drapery proposals for the Oval Office, and this simple treatment of straight-falling panels from steel rods was approved by both President and Mrs. Kennedy. Even though John F. Kennedy was ever conscious about using American products, these draperies were in fact designed and manufactured in Paris. Courtesy Paul Manno. Photo: Jim Frank.

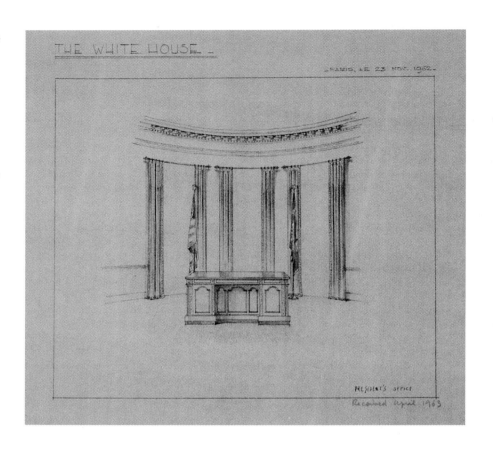

For the floor, Boudin and the President selected a red carpet, somewhat to the disappointment of Jacqueline Kennedy. "I know the President loves a red rug," wrote the First Lady to the chief usher, "but ask Boudin if he does not think it too obvious (or banal? In French) to do Pres. Office in red, white and blue."[3] The President's choice remained red. "We will supply and install a specially made dark red oval rug for the President's Office," recorded Jansen in a May 1, 1963, estimate, which "will be made in the United States, as requested."[4]

Other aspects of the room's decor were decided later. The First Lady had wanted to retain the off-white walls, but inevitably the color of the yet-to-be-installed draperies dictated a change to pure white. The slipcovered sofas also had to be changed; Jacqueline Kennedy was quick to note that "we can't make . . . [them] white."[5] Boudin subsequently proposed red leather for "recovering the 2 existing sofas which are now in cream,"[6] although this concept does not seem to have received the First Lady's final approval. For the fireplace, she planned to utilize the then-still-unused green and white marble

The Oval Office, looking toward the windows, November 23, 1963. In this view the draperies and carpet selected by the President and Stéphane Boudin are shown just after their installation. Courtesy John F. Kennedy Library.

mantelpiece originally purchased for the Yellow Oval Room. "We tried the French eagle mantel in the President's office," described the White House curator in a September 1962 memorandum to the First Lady, "and since it is much smaller than the one already there, installing it will be a major job which will probably take more time than the President will be away. Could we hold up on this until you are away at Christmas?"[7] The existing mantel, dating from the Taft administration, was subsequently retained, while the

The Oval Office as it appeared on November 23, 1963, after the installation of the new draperies and carpet by Jansen. Courtesy John F. Kennedy Library.

French mantel, which was presumably deemed too small for the President's office, was incorporated in the coinciding redecoration of the State floor's Family Dining Room.

Completion of the majority of work was scheduled for late November 1963, when the President and First Lady would be campaigning in Texas. While the Kennedys were greeted in San Antonio, Fort Worth, and then

"The White House Cabinet Room." Jansen's proposal for the alteration of the lunette transom over the door leading to the Oval Office, July 19, 1962. Jansen recommended the inclusion of mirrored glass above the door and for the adjacent bookcases. Courtesy Paul Manno. Photo: Jim Frank.

Dallas, the Oval Office was painted and the new window treatments and carpet were installed. Unfortunately, the President never saw the finished room, nor did the First Lady. Following a private Mass for the slain President's family, Jacqueline Kennedy walked to the Oval Office, only to find John F. Kennedy's possessions already removed to make way for those of the new President, Lyndon B. Johnson. Mrs. Kennedy, wrote J. B. West, "never got to see the effect of the room she and Boudin had worked so carefully to perfect. . . ."[8]

THE CABINET ROOM

Unable to appreciate the completed Oval Office, Jacqueline Kennedy went on to the nearby Cabinet Room. There she sat down to admire a more complete example of Boudin's designs for the late President.

As he had for the redecoration of the Oval Office, Stéphane Boudin dedicated over a year and a half to the formulation of the new Cabinet Room. He proposed numerous alterations to the architecture, including a new mantelpiece. However, not all of the Frenchman's proposals were accepted. Among the approved changes were a series of false transoms for above the doors and bookcases, opposite the wall of arched French doors. Made of mirrored glass, these false windows increased the available light while they provided a greater formality and sense of symmetry with regard to the room's overall architecture. The changes were subtle, requiring even the First Lady to note that "I don't know what's new but I like all."[9]

For the actual windows, Boudin designed straight-falling drapery panels finished with demi-lune valances. These were made of yellow striped silk and suspended in a manner similar to the Oval Office treatment. Presumably the valance design for the Cabinet Room draperies was also similar to what

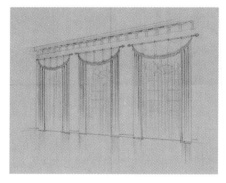

TOP: *Jansen's proposal for the alteration of the mantel wall in the Cabinet Room, July 19, 1962. Courtesy Paul Manno. Photo: Jim Frank.* CENTER: *Detail of Jansen's proposal for the mantel wall treatment in the Cabinet Room, July 17, 1962. Courtesy Paul Manno. Photo: Jim Frank.* BOTTOM: *"The White House Cabinet Room." Proposal for new draperies for the Cabinet Room by Jansen's Paris office, dated April 1963. Courtesy Paul Manno. Photo: Jim Frank.*

Boudin had proposed for the Oval Office but which the First Lady had deemed "a bit feminine for Pres. office"[10] and hence subsequently canceled.

Another addition to the Cabinet Room was a new carpet, again selected by Boudin. A stock design from Stark Carpet Corporation of New York, the green, gold, ivory, and brown "Directoire" carpet was based on early-nineteenth-century French and English lattice-patterned designs. Its installation actually preceded the President's trip to Texas, so it was one of the few aspects of the decorative scheme John F. Kennedy actually saw implemented.

Like makeovers of the State-floor rooms, the redecoration of the Oval Office and Cabinet Room was intended to provide an accurate representation of the Kennedy style or aesthetic. However, these rooms were more complete translations of the taste, aspirations, and ideals of John F. Kennedy than were the Red, Blue, and Green rooms because less of the formulation of their respective decors had to be based upon historical context or precedent. Indeed, Sister Parish's redecoration of the Oval Office in early 1961 conveyed the President's well-known love of the sea and all things nautical with little reference to prior occupants of the room. The Parish decor also promoted a youthfulness as well as a somewhat informal Cape Cod comfortableness; it was a successful translation of how President Kennedy wanted to be seen, particularly in contrast to his predecessor, Dwight D. Eisenhower, who was nearly thirty years his senior and very much the orderly, "by the book" West Pointer.

The subsequent Boudin redecoration of the Oval Office and the nearby Cabinet Room reflected a maturing Kennedy Presidency. Indeed, by late 1962 the term *New Frontier*—defined by candidate Kennedy during his 1960 acceptance speech for his party's Presidential nomination—was no longer actively used to describe the administration. The youngest elected American president had grown into an established statesman, and the New Frontier informality of Sister Parish's decor was therefore in need of replacement. Surely Boudin's more cosmopolitan scheme was intended to better represent the global image of the mediator of the October 1962 Cuban missile crisis and the formulator of the 1963 Nuclear Test Ban Treaty.

The President's evolution as a world leader, as well as his personal involvement in the planning of a new Oval Office, provide possible reasons why a reproduction of the room was not part of the John F. Kennedy Presidential Library from the time plans began in 1964. Indeed, recreations of

President Lyndon Johnson shown in the recently redecorated Cabinet Room during a presentation ceremony in 1964. Stéphane Boudin's draperies, carpeting, and mirrored glass transom are visible. Courtesy John F. Kennedy Library.

other Presidents' offices had become popular and therefore standard features of their respective libraries and museums by that time. In fact, in April 1963 the First Lady began inquiring about reproducing the "Resolute" desk for just such an installation in a yet-to-be-planned Kennedy library; her interest in the desk suggested a strong desire to illustrate for posterity the backdrop then being formulated for the Kennedy Presidency. However, the assassination of the President in November 1963 presumably changed her thinking. Jacqueline Kennedy may have recognized that a recreation of her husband's Oval Office would have to depict the earlier decor and not the long-planned, more sophisticated Boudin collaboration that the President never had the opportunity to use. Presumably in recognition of this fact, the former First Lady decided against a full reproduction of the Oval Office.

The Legacy

When the Kennedy administration came to its abrupt end, with it closed the vigorous campaign waged by Jacqueline Kennedy to restore historical integrity and beauty to the White House interiors. By that time the State Rooms on the ground and first floors were, for the most part, completed. A few finishing details previously arranged for by Mrs. Kennedy were completed in the months following her departure from the White House. The rooms changed very little during the Johnson administration, in part due to their recent redecoration but also in reverence to the fallen President and in honor of Jacqueline Kennedy's great efforts on behalf of their restoration. The catastrophic national event of the President's assassination and the jarring image of his widow leaving the White House sanctified these rooms, in a sense, delaying the inevitable change that comes to all public residences.

Lady Bird Johnson took a special interest in preserving the work of Mrs. Kennedy, building on the foundation left by her predecessor. In the new edition of the White House guidebook she retained the original introduction written by Jacqueline Kennedy, adding her own remarks after those of the previous First Lady. The formation of the Committee for the Preservation of the White House in 1964 served to carry on the work started by Mrs. Kennedy and the Fine Arts Committee. Both Jacqueline Kennedy and Henry du Pont were appointed members; however, by that time the quest to acquire period furnishings for the White House had subsided and the activity of this new committee was largely ceremonial. Du Pont continued to maintain a rela-

LEFT AND FOLLOWING PAGES: *Jacqueline Kennedy leaving the White House for the last time on December 6, 1963. She is shown exiting through the East Garden, which was then in the process of being redesigned by Rachel Lambert Mellon. When completed by President and Mrs. Johnson, the garden was renamed the Jacqueline Kennedy Garden. Courtesy John F. Kennedy Library.*

tionship with the committee, and with the Office of the White House Curator, as an advisor until his health began to fail in the late 1960s.

Eventually the Kennedy White House interiors were altered. By the end of the decade a new philosophy regarding historic interiors was being formulated. The tastes and methods of Stéphane Boudin, as well as those of Henry du Pont, were replaced with new opinions, knowledge, and scholarship. On viewing the Blue Room in 1970, an architectural historian, possibly Edward Vason Jones, was quoted as saying he "had forgotten this room was so . . . unattractive."[1] Jones, along with others including Berry Tracy of the Metropolitan Museum of Art, was challenging the establishment with regard to historic interiors. Where Boudin's decorations had been inspired by period documents, the work of Jones, who ultimately redecorated the Blue Room during the Nixon administration, was seen as a "precise recreation."[2] The difference between the two is actually what historian William Seale defined as "the historic interior recreated for purposes of illustration [versus] the adapted interior . . . preserved for modern use."[3] Boudin's interiors were not intended as museum installations but as living environments, albeit with an historical context.

If Stéphane Boudin did capture the reflections of the Kennedys in his decoration of the State Rooms, then he succeeded as a decorator. Recent Presidents and First Ladies publicly expressing admiration for one or both of the Kennedys have paid homage to them by reviving some of Boudin's designs. Nancy Reagan sought to duplicate Boudin's placement of a center table in the Blue Room. She also copied his arrangement of sofas and chairs in the Yellow Oval Room and returned the portrait of Benjamin Franklin to its Kennedy-era position over the mantel in the Green Room. "I think Mrs. Reagan wants to capture some of the elegance of the Kennedy decor,"[4] assessed James Ketchum in 1985. The Clintons have continued to encourage this reevaluation of Boudin's work. The 1995 redecoration of the Blue Room included a paper border representing a continuous blue fabric valance as well as the placement of a table in the center of the room, suggesting a distinct link to the Frenchman's earlier scheme.[5]

The influence of Stéphane Boudin's presidential commission was, and is, not limited to the Presidential residence. The textile reproductions based on the period documents that he supplied for the Red and Blue rooms remain popular choices of museum curators and private collectors seeking to recreate an early-nineteenth-century aesthetic. The Frenchman's interpretations of

post-Civil War interiors in the White House—bold and bright with sharp contrasts of color and pattern—led other museums away from the inappropriate pale palettes of Colonial Revival theorists. Equally valid is the recognition that Boudin's White House work was instrumental in creating one of the most dramatic backdrops ever created for a Presidency, helping to expand what had been up until that time a very conservative decorating spectrum in America. Although not a native of this country, Stéphane Boudin, through his work in the Kennedy White House, played an important role in the development of a general appreciation for American period and contemporary decorative arts.

Defining Henry du Pont's influence on the White House during the Kennedy administration requires looking beyond the newspaper headlines and press releases. Crucial to the success of the project, he fulfilled his role as honorary leader of the Fine Arts Committee. By agreeing to serve he helped claim historical authenticity as the goal of the restoration project. The presence of Stéphane Boudin and Jacqueline Kennedy's affinity for interiors that reflected fashion as well as historical accuracy prevented du Pont from having absolute control over the appearance of the rooms. The Kennedy restoration was a collaborative effort from the beginning, and Henry du Pont understood this. John Sweeney recalls that the venerable collector felt truly honored to be asked to contribute his opinions to the White House project; in so doing his own knowledge was validated, along with his life's work creating the museum at Winterthur. Any sense of disappointment or frustration on his part at being overruled by other contributors was outweighed by his pride in being part of the historic project. In spite of the aesthetic and philosophical conflicts between du Pont and Boudin, their unofficial, and certainly unacknowledged, collaboration created the legacy of historicism and glamour that surrounds the Kennedy White House.

Overall, the work of Henry du Pont's Fine Arts Committee between 1961 and 1963 was impressive. Although many of the details of room decoration were ultimately chosen by Stéphane Boudin, the committee defined the historical parameters of the restoration, determining the most appropriate period of interpretation for the State Rooms—decisions that continue to guide the decoration of the White House to the present day. Furthermore, the formation of the committee and the responsible leadership it represented enabled the passage of the act designating the White House a museum, preserving forever its contents as a nationally owned permanent collection under the supervision of a professional curator. Committee members' collective efforts yielded over five hundred new acquisitions for the White House, including 129 chairs, 82 tables, 50 lighting fixtures, and 7 mantels.[6] However, the Fine Arts Committee's most significant contribution falls in the realm of public perception. The academically guided committee created the impression that the restoration was guided by organization and expertise, generating public support and enthusiasm for the work of Jacqueline Kennedy and setting a precedent for all such future endeavors in the White House.

More than any collector, decorator, or historian, Jacqueline Kennedy was most responsible for the transformation of the White House interiors between 1961 and 1963. Her interest in the history and furnishing of the executive mansion drove the project from its inception, and her attention to detail in each room is evident through the voluminous written record of the project. In spite of the inaccuracies that plague any attempt to create authentic period interiors, Jacqueline Kennedy's efforts set a high academic standard. It was her vision that inspired the commitment to excellence in the decoration of the White House that continues long after her residence. She will forever be remembered as the First Lady who brought history and beauty to the President's house. More than thirty years after its brief existence, the Kennedy White House continues to intrigue the American public. The glamorous and stately settings that both President and Mrs. Kennedy created form the backdrop in the American memory of the enduring image of Camelot.

Appendix

Illustrations by Robert Bentley Adams, AIA

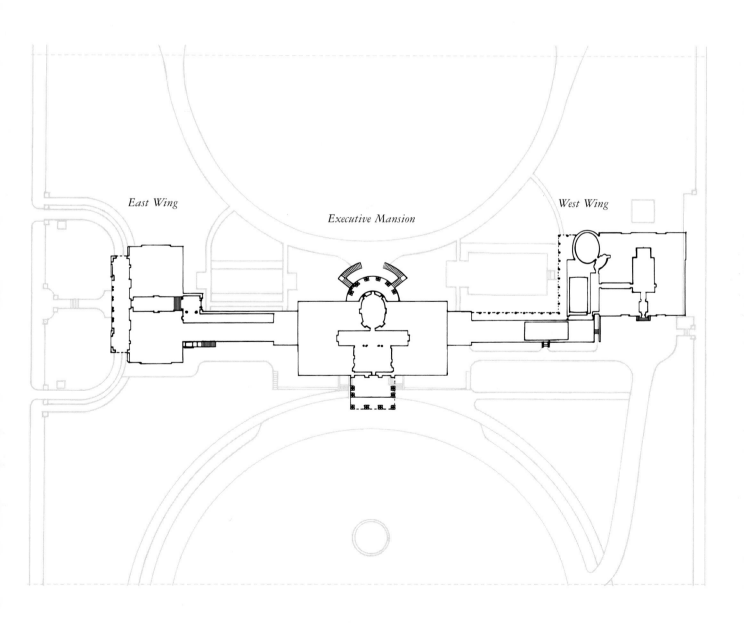

East Wing

Executive Mansion

West Wing

GROUND FLOOR

A   *Hall*

B   *Library*

C   *Vermeil Room*

D   *China Room*

E   *Diplomatic Reception Room*

F   *Map Room/Curator's Office*

G   *Kitchen*

H   *Old Kitchen/Restoration Upholstery Shop*

a   *East Colonnade to Theater and East Wing*

b   *West Colonnade to Pool and West Wing*

c   *Service Driveway*

FIRST FLOOR

A   *North Entrance Hall*

B   *Cross Hall*

C   *East Room*

D   *State Dining Room*

E   *Green Room*

F   *Blue Room*

G   *Red Room*

H   *Family Dining Room*

a   *North Portico*

b   *South Portico*

c   *East Terrace*

d   *West Terrace*

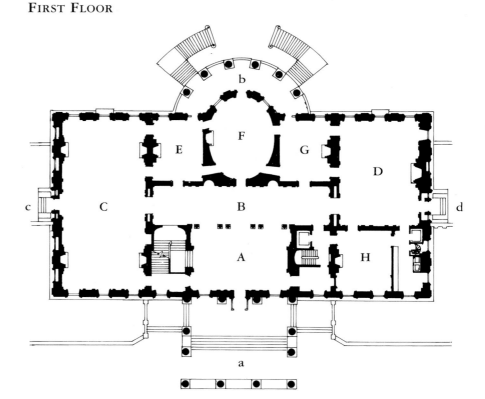

SECOND FLOOR

A   *Queens' Bedroom*

B   *Queens' Sitting Room*

C   *West Sitting or Monroe Hall*

D   *Lincoln Sitting Room*

E   *Lincoln Bedroom*

F   *Treaty Room*

G   *Yellow Oval Room*

H   *Cross Hall*

I   *Family Quarters*

a   *Truman Balcony*

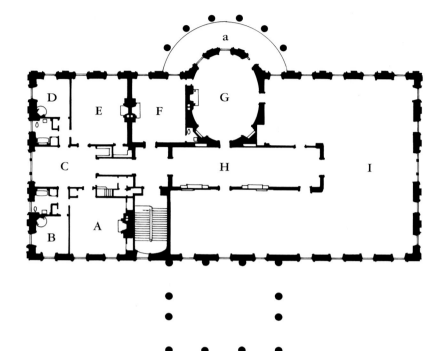

THIRD FLOOR

A   *Cross Hall*

B   *Solarium / School Classroom*

C   *West Solarium Nursery School*

D   *Empire (Red Toile) Guest Bedroom*

E   *Pineapple Sitting Room*

F   *Pineapple Guest Bedroom*

G   *Country Guest Bedroom*

H   *(Orange Blossom) Chintz Bedroom*

I   *Blue Toile Guest Bedroom*

J   *Sitting Room*

K   *North Double Guest Bedroom*

L   *Servants' Quarters*

a   *Promenade Terrace*

b   *Fernery Greenhouse*

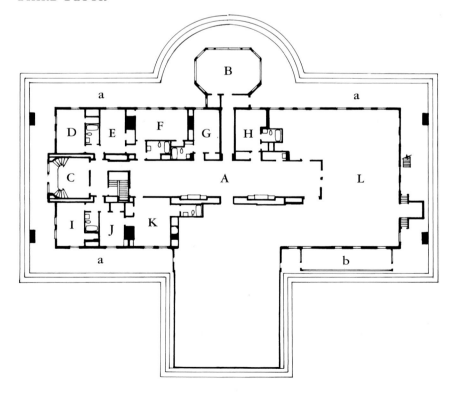

WEST WING

A   *Oval Office*

B   *Cabinet Room*

C   *Swimming Pool*

D   *Secretary's Room*

E   *Fish Room*

F   *Lobby*

G   *Offices*

H   *Service areas*

a   *Rose Garden*

b   *Colonnade*

c   *Visitor's Entrance*

d   *Connecting Lobby to Ground Floor*

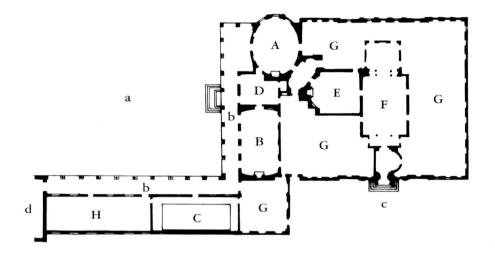

Endnotes

CHAPTER ONE

1   Douglas Cater, "The Kennedy Look in the Arts," *Horizon,* Vol. IV, No. 1, (September 1961): 5.

2   Ruth Montgomery, "She's Zestful at Work or Play," *Philadelphia Inquirer,* 7 March 1962.

3   Robert Frost, as quoted in Douglas Cater, "The Kennedy Look in the Arts," *Horizon,* Vol. IV, No. 1, (September 1961): 5.

4   Hugh Sidey, "The First Lady Brings History and Beauty to the White House," *Life* (1 September 1961): 62.

CHAPTER TWO

1   William Seale, *The President's House: A History,* Vol. 1 (Washington, D.C.: White House Historical Association, 1986), 864–869. Seale's comprehensive study of the history of the White House is the basis for this discussion of the Coolidge redecoration. This two-volume work contains a complete discussion of the decorating campaigns in the White House through the Truman Administration.

2   J. B. West, *Upstairs at the White House: My Life with the First Ladies* (New York: Coward, McCann & Geoghegan, 1973), 198–200.

3   Mary Van Rennsselaer Thayer, *Jacqueline Kennedy: The White House Years* (Boston: Little, Brown and Company, 1971), 282.

4   For a complete discussion of the life of Henry Francis du Pont and of the development of the Winterthur Museum, several sources are invaluable. Jay E. Cantor's *Winterthur* (New York: Harry N. Abrams, 1985) is the largest and most comprehensive description of Mr. du Pont, his collections, and the Winterthur estate. Volume I of *Winterthur Portfolio* (Winterthur, Delaware: The Henry Francis du Pont Winterthur Museum, Inc., 1964) contains several important essays by members of the Winterthur curatorial and education staffs. In particular, John A.H. Sweeney's "The Evolution of the Winterthur Rooms (pp. 106–129) describes Mr. du Pont's development of the period rooms at Winterthur and his design aesthetic. Other important writings on these subjects by Sweeney are "Henry Francis du Pont: The Growth of a Collector," *Arts in Virginia,* 19, No. 3 (Spring 1979), 18–31; *The Treasure House of Early American Rooms* (New York: Viking Press, 1963); and *Winterthur Illustrated* (Winterthur, Delaware: The Henry Francis du Pont Winterthur Museum, 1963).

5   Henry Francis du Pont to Harlan B. Phillips, typescript of interview, April 1962, "The Reminiscences of Henry F. du Pont." Archives, Winterthur Museum, Garden and Library (hereafter called Winterthur Archives), Winterthur, Delaware, 8.

6   Henry du Pont to Jacqueline Kennedy, 9 March 1961, Winterthur Archives, Box 1310.

7   Ibid.

8   Hugh Sidey, "The First Lady Brings History and Beauty to the White House," *Life* (1 September 1961): 62.

9   Julian Boyd and Lyman Butterfield, "The White House as a Symbol," 24 April 1961, 3.

10   Sidey, 62.

11   Jane Engelhard to Henry du Pont, undated [February 1961], Winterthur Archives.

12   Jacqueline Kennedy to Henry du Pont, 11 March 1961, Winterthur Archives, Box 451.

[13] William Voss Elder III to Ronald Grele, 15 December 1965. Typescript of interview. William Voss Elder III, personal papers.

[14] *An act concerning the White House and providing for the care and preservation of its historic and artistic contents.* 87th Congress, 1st session, Serial 2422 (15 August 1961) Public Law 87–286, approved September 22, 1961.

[15] John A. H. Sweeney to Lorraine Waxman Pearce, 5 May 1961, Winterthur Archives, Box 1310.

[16] Charles Hummel to Elaine M. Rice, personal communication, 10 March 1993.

[17] Henry du Pont to Lorraine Waxman Pearce, 22 November 1961, Winterthur Archives, Box. 1310.

[18] Lorraine Waxman Pearce to Henry du Pont, 13 December 1961, Winterthur Archives, Box 433.

[19] William Voss Elder III to Ronald H. Grele, 15 December 1965. Transcript of interview. Private collection.

[20] Maxine Cheshire, "They Never Introduce M. Boudin," *Washington Post,* 9 September 1962.

[21] Paul Manno to James Archer Abbott, interview in New York City, 23 April 1996.

[22] Jacqueline Kennedy to Henry du Pont, 11 November 1962. Winterthur Archives, Box 451.

[23] William Voss Elder III to Jacqueline Kennedy, 20 July 1962. Private collection.

[24] William Voss Elder III to Jacqueline Kennedy, 29 November 1962. Private collection.

[25] William Voss Elder III to Elaine M. Rice, personal communication, 12 March 1993.

[26] Lorraine Waxman Pearce to Elaine M. Rice, personal communication, 5 February 1993.

[27] Marvin D. Schwartz to Henry du Pont, 2 June 1961, Winterthur Archives, Box 433.

[28] James Biddle to Henry du Pont, 2 June 1961, Winterthur Archives, Box 433.

[29] Lorraine Waxman Pearce to Henry du Pont, 8 August 1962, Winterthur Archives, Box 433.

[30] William Voss Elder III to Elaine M. Rice, personal communication, 12 March 1993.

[31] Jacqueline Kennedy to Henry du Pont, 20 September 1962, Winterthur Archives. In this letter, written while at sea awaiting the start of the America's Cup Race, Jacqueline Kennedy expresses her anger over the series of articles by Maxine Cheshire and her extreme disappointment that those close to the project, like Franco Scalamandré, were persuaded to divulge information about the White House restoration. She also discusses Lorraine Pearce's desire for publicity as the primary reason that she was unable to continue in her role as Curator and praises William Elder for his discretion and professionalism in dealing with the issues publicized by Cheshire.

[32] William Voss Elder III to Henry du Pont, 15 January 1963. Private collection

[33] Ibid.

[34] Henry du Pont to William Voss Elder III, 17 January 1963. Private collection.

[35] John A. H. Sweeney to Elaine M. Rice, personal communication, November 1996.

[36] Columbia Broadcasting System, *It Was an Unprecedented Seven Days of Television . . . February 14, 15, 16, 17, 18, 19, 20,* n.d., Winterthur Archives, Box 298A. Booklet, 1962.

[37] Maxine Cheshire, "The First Lady and the White House," *Newsweek,* 17 September, 1962: 72.

CHAPTER THREE

[1] Diana Vreeland, *D.V.* (New York: Alfred A. Knopf, 1984), 170.

[2] "Toward the Ideal," *Time,* Vol. 82, No. 10 (September 6, 1963): 67.

3   Mark Hampton, *Legendary Decorators of the Twentieth Century* (New York: Doubleday, 1992), 168.

4   John Cornforth, "Boudin at Leeds Castle—I," *Country Life* No. 14 (April 1983): 925.

5   John Walker, *Self-Portrait with Donors* (Boston: Little, Brown and Company, 1974), 255.

6   Ibid, 256.

7   Paul Manno to James Abbott, Interview held in New York City, 23 April 1996.

8   Milton Brackner, "Parisian Assesses White House Decor," *New York Times* Vol. 49, 1 April 1961, sec. 1, A1.

9   Jayne Wrightsman to Sister Parish, 16 June 1961. Collection of Parish-Hadley, New York City.

10 Jayne Wrightsman to Sister Parish, 18 July 1961. Collection of Parish-Hadley, New York City.

11 Paul Manno to J. B. West, 17 June 1963. Private Collection.

12 Carl Sferrazza Anthony, "Love, Jackie," *Forbes American Heritage,* Vol. 45, No. 5 (September 1994): 98.

13 Stéphane Boudin to J. B. West, 23 April 1963. Private Collection.

14 J. B. West, *Upstairs at the White House: My Life with the First Ladies* (New York: Coward, McCann & Geoghegan, 1973), 246.

15 Stéphane Boudin to J. B. West, 14 March 1963. Private Collection.

16 Paul Manno to James Abbott, Interview held in New York City, 23 April 1996.

17 Hampton, 179.

18 Martin Filler, "A Clash of Tastes at the White House," *New York Times Magazine* (November 2, 1980): 89.

CHAPTER FOUR

1   Perry Wolf, *A Tour of the White House with Mrs. John F. Kennedy* (Garden City, New York: Doubleday & Company, 1962), 101.

2 Henry du Pont to Jayne Wrightsman, 22 November 1961, Winterthur Archives.

3 Anne H. Lincoln, *The Kennedy White House Parties* (New York Viking Press, 1967), 12.

CHAPTER FIVE

1 Perry Wolff, *A Tour of the White House with Mrs. John F. Kennedy* (Garden City, New York: Doubleday & Company, Inc., 1962), 79.

2 Mary Van Rensselaer Thayer, *Jacqueline Kennedy: The White House Years* (Boston: Little, Brown and Company, 1971), 133.

3 Ibid.

4 Jansen, Invoice No. 3741, 17 January 1963. Private Collection.

5 Jansen, Invoice No. 3825, 9 July 1963. Private Collection.

6 J. B. West, *Upstairs at the White House: My Life with the First Ladies* (New York: Coward, McCann & Geoghegan, 1973), 131.

7 Jansen, "Notes Concerning the White House," 14 February 1963. Private Collection.

8 Ibid.

9 Paul Manno to J. B. West, 3 June 1963. Private Collection.

10 Ibid.

11 Thayer, 134.

12 Jansen, Estimate No. 161.660, 13 April 1964. Private Collection.

13 Ibid.

14 Thayer, 134.

CHAPTER SIX

1 Mrs. Kennedy's preference for French design influenced the concentration on the descriptive title "American Empire." Many of the furniture forms utilized by early-nineteenth-century American cabinetmakers were borrowed from French Empire pattern books. However, Charles

Montgomery, director of the Winterthur fellowship program and a leading authority on American neoclassical furniture, referred to the American interpretations of French Empire as part of the "Late Federal" period. Other scholars agreed with this classification. Francophiles like Mrs. Kennedy continued to utilize the stronger French association.

2 Although their 1902 decorative scheme for the Red Room was eclectic overall, McKim, Mead, and White did try to focus on the French Empire. Following the cue set by the Monroe mantel, the Beaux-Arts–trained architects included a large Empire-style display cabinet along the room's east wall. This piece was quite large and included an array of ormolu mounts worthy of any piece of furniture commissioned for Napoleon.

3 John A. H. Sweeney to Henry F. du Pont, 31 May 1961. Winterthur Archives.

4 Henry du Pont had been offered the Lannuier guéridon for the collections at Winterthur. However, he passed due to his belief that the table was too eccentric in its design. After the table entered the White House, du Pont often told others that "that table is my greatest mistake." He regretted ever rejecting the piece. John A. H. Sweeney, former Curator of the Henry Francis du Pont Winterthur Museum, to James Abbott interview held at Philipsburg Manor, North Tarrytown, New York, April 1987.

5 Paul Manno to James Abbott, interview held in New York City, 10 May 1996.

6 Jayne Wrightsman to Sister Parish, 28 June 1961. Collection of Parish-Hadley, New York City.

7 Stéphane Boudin to Mrs. John Pearce (Lorraine Waxman Pearce), 5 July 1961. Winterthur Archives.

8 Henry Francis du Pont to Lorraine Waxman Pearce, 3 August 1961. Winterthur Archives.

9 Jacqueline Kennedy to Sister Parish, undated. Collection of Parish-Hadley, New York City.

[10] Henry Francis du Pont to Lorraine Waxman Pearce, 3 August 1961. Winterthur Archives.

[11] Scalamandré received numerous inquiries regarding the textiles produced from the Boudin-supplied documents. At first, the fabric was not available. "This is to certify that the fabric we made for the Red Room of the White House is not for sale; either in the same color or in a different color," stated a Scalamandré memorandum. Later the fabrics became special order, accessible to all. Museums throughout the country incorporated the cerise and gold textiles into their decorative schemes.

[12] Jacqueline Kennedy to Sister Parish, undated. Collection of Parish-Hadley, New York City.

[13] Mary Van Rensselaer Thayer, *Jacqueline Kennedy: The White House Years* (Boston: Little, Brown and Company, 1971), 133.

[14] J. B. West, *Upstairs at the White House: My Life with the First Ladies* (New York: Coward, McCann & Geoghegan, 1973), 246.

[15] Boudin had the sconces from the 1952 redecoration raised about a foot to incorporate the hanging of portraits. This was not continued once the walls were recovered. At that time the sconces were removed. This method of picture-hanging—below sconces—was utilized by Boudin when the Blue Room was redecorated in late 1962. A similar arrangement was used by Boudin in Lady Baillie's bedroom at Leeds Castle.

CHAPTER SEVEN

[1] J. B. West, *Upstairs at the White House: My Life with the First Ladies* (New York: Coward, McCann & Geoghegan, 1973), 252.

[2] Henry F. du Pont to Jacqueline Kennedy, 7 October 1961. Winterthur Archives.

[3] Ibid.

[4] Henry F. du Pont to Jacqueline Kennedy, 29 May 1961. Winterthur Archives.

[5] Jacqueline Kennedy to Henry F. du Pont, 20 September 1962. Winterthur Archives.

6   James Roe Ketchum to James Abbott, interview held in Washington, D.C., 29 May 1985.

7   West, 243.

8   Franco Scalamandré to Jayne Wrightsman, 4 June 1962. Scalamandré Archives.

9   This sample exists in two pieces, one of which is in the collection of the John F. Kennedy Library. The second section, which maintains its Scalamandré identification tag, is in a private collection.

10 Jayne Wrightsman to Franco Scalamandré, 5 July 1962. Scalamandré Archives.

11 Jansen, Invoice No. 3740, 17 January 1963. Private collection.

12 Jansen, "Notes Concerning the White House," 14 February 1963. Private collection.

13 Ibid.

CHAPTER EIGHT

1   Martin Filler, "A Clash of Tastes at the White House," *New York Times Magazine* (November 2, 1980): 89.

2   Clement Conger to James Abbott, 13 March 1985. Author's collection.

3   Paul Manno to James Abbott, interview held in New York City, 23 April 1996.

4   Jacqueline Kennedy to Paul Manno, 23 June 1961. Private Collection.

5   Henry F. du Pont to Jacqueline Kennedy, 14 June 1961. Winterthur Archives.

6   Henry F. du Pont to Gertrude Carroway, 21 July 1961. Winterthur Archives.

7   J. B. West, *Upstairs at the White House: My Life with the First Ladies* (New York: Coward, McCann & Geoghegan, 1973), 246.

8   John Pearce to James Abbott, telephone interview, 3 March 1997.

9   William Voss Elder III to J. B. West, 17 July 1962. Private Collection.

[10] William Voss Elder III to Jacqueline Kennedy, 1 June 1962. Private Collection.

[11] Filler, 89.

[12] Janet G. Felton to Franco Scalamandré, 30 January 1962. Scalamandré Archives.

[13] Conover Hunt-Jones, *Dolley and the "Great Little Madison"* (Washington, D.C.: American Institute of Architects Foundation, 1977), 37.

[14] Janet G. Felton to Franco Scalamandré, 8 February 1962. Scalamandré Archives.

[15] Jayne Wrightsman to Franco Scalamandré, 29 May 1962. Scalamandré Archives.

[16] William Voss Elder III to Jacqueline Kennedy, 3 August 1962. Private Collection.

[17] William Voss Elder III to Jacqueline Kennedy, 16 August 1962. Private Collection.

[18] Jacqueline Kennedy to William V. Elder III, 23 August 1962. Private Collection.

[19] Marguerite Jardel, "Tassinari and Châtel: 1762–1962," *La Revue Française* No. 137 (February 1962): supplement.

[20] Henry du Pont to Jayne Wrightsman, 22 January 1963. Winterthur Archives.

[21] Filler, 89.

CHAPTER NINE

[1] "People," *Time* Vol. LXXVIII, No. 16 (October 20, 1961): 38.

[2] Ibid.

[3] "New Look in the White House," *Look* Vol. 26, No. 1 (January 2, 1962): 26.

[4] Henry du Pont to Jacqueline Kennedy, 2 May 1961. Winterthur Archives. Richard Howland was the President of the National Trust for

Historic Preservation as well as an architectural historian who provided guidance for the White House project.

5   Henry du Pont to Cornelia Conger, 8 May 1961. Winterthur Archives.

6   Mrs. Francis Henry Lenygon, Chairman of the National Committee on Historic Preservation, to Henry du Pont, 21 August 1961. Winterthur Archives.

7   Mary Van Rensselaer Thayer, *Jacqueline Kennedy: The White House Years* (Boston: Little, Brown and Company, 1971), 291.

8   Jansen, "Notes Concerning the White House," 14 February 1963. Private Collection.

9   Ibid.

10   Ibid.

11   Ibid.

12   Ibid.

13   Jansen, "Notes Concerning the White House," 16 October 1963. Private Collection.

14   Martin Filler, "A Clash of Tastes at the White House," *New York Times Magazine* (November 2, 1980): 89.

CHAPTER TEN

1   J. B. West, *Upstairs at the White House: My Life with the First Ladies* (New York: Coward, McCann & Geoghegan, 1973), 200.

2   Mary Van Rensselaer Thayer, *Jacqueline Kennedy: The White House Years* (Boston: Little, Brown and Company, 1971), 347.

3   Jansen, "Notes Concerning The White House," February 14, 1963. Private Collection.

4   Ibid.

5   Jansen, Estimate No. 101.557, 20 March 1963. Private Collection.

6   Oleg Cassini, *A Thousand Days of Magic: Dressing Jacqueline Kennedy for the White House* (New York: Rizzoli International Publications, 1996), 69.

7   Thayer, 130.

8   Henry F. du Pont to Jayne Wrightsman, 22 November 1961. Winterthur Archives.

9   William Voss Elder III to Jacqueline Kennedy, 25 March 1963. Private Collection.

10 Henry F. du Pont to Jayne Wrightsman, 3 July 1961. Winterthur Archives.

11 Ibid.

12 West, 203.

CHAPTER ELEVEN

1   Jacqueline Kennedy to Sister Parish, 19 September 1961. Collection of Parish-Hadley, New York City.

2   Sister Parish to Jacqueline Kennedy, 16 September 1961. Collection of Parish-Hadley, New York City.

3   Henry F. du Pont to Jayne Wrightsman, 22 November 1961. Winterthur Archives.

4   Jayne Wrightsman to Sister Parish, 28 June 1961. Collection of Parish-Hadley, New York City.

5   J. B. West, *Upstairs at the White House: My Life with the First Ladies* (New York: Coward, McCann & Geoghegan, 1973), 277.

CHAPTER TWELVE

1   Mary Van Rensselaer Thayer, *Jacqueline Kennedy: The White House Years* (Boston: Little, Brown and Company, 1971), 251.

2   Jayne Wrightsman to Sister Parish, 18 July 1961. Collection of Parish-Hadley, New York City.

3   Ibid.

4   Jacqueline Kennedy to Sister Parish, 30 June 1961. Collection of Parish-Hadley, New York City.

[5] Jacqueline Kennedy to Sister Parish, 17 July 1961. Collection of Parish-Hadley, New York City.

[6] Jayne Wrightsman to Jacqueline Kennedy, undated. Collection of Parish-Hadley, New York City.

[7] Sister Parish to Jacqueline Kennedy, 16 September 1961. Collection of Parish-Hadley, New York City.

[8] Jayne Wrightsman to Sister Parish, 16 June 1961. Collection of Parish-Hadley, New York City.

[9] Ibid.

[10] Jayne Wrightsman to Sister Parish, 18 July 1961. Collection of Parish-Hadley, New York City.

[11] Thayer, 252.

[12] Jayne Wrightsman to Sister Parish, 28 June 1961. Collection of Parish-Hadley, New York City.

[13] Paul Manno to James Abbott, interview held in New York City, 23 April 1996.

[14] Jansen, Invoice No. 3779, 17 April 1963. Private collection.

[15] Jansen, Estimate No. 101.556, 8 March 1963. Private collection.

[16] Jacqueline Kennedy to Sister Parish, undated. Collection of Parish-Hadley, New York City.

[17] Jacqueline Kennedy to Sister Parish, undated. Collection of Parish-Hadley, New York City.

[18] West, 270.

[19] Thayer, 252.

[20] Thayer, 251.

CHAPTER THIRTEEN

[1] Mary Van Rensselaer Thayer, *Jacqueline Kennedy: The White House Years* (Boston: Little, Brown and Company, 1971), 37.

[2] William Voss Elder III to Jacqueline Kennedy, 29 November 1962. Private Collection.

3   Henry F. du Pont to William Voss Elder III, 17 January 1963. Private Collection.

4   Henry F. du Pont to Jacqueline Kennedy, 15 December 1962. Winterthur Archives.

5   Jacqueline Kennedy to Henry F. du Pont, 20 December 1962. Winterthur Archives.

6   Rose Fitzgerald Kennedy, *Times to Remember* (New York: Bantam Books, 1975), 427.

7   Jaqueline Kennedy to William Voss Elder III, undated. Private Collection.

CHAPTER FOURTEEN

1   Mary Van Rensselaer Thayer, *Jacqueline Kennedy: The White House Years* (Boston: Little, Brown and Company, 1971), 38.

2   James Roe Ketchum to James Abbott, interview held in Washington, D.C., 29 May 1985.

3   William Voss Elder III to Jacqueline Kennedy, 24 June 1963. Private collection.

4   Jansen, "Notes Concerning the White House," 14 February 1963. Private collection.

5   William Voss Elder III to Jacqueline Kennedy, 20 February 1963. Private collection.

6   Perry Wolff, *A Tour of the White House with Mrs. John F. Kennedy* (Garden City, New York: Doubleday & Company, 1962), 222.

7   Ibid.

CHAPTER FIFTEEN

1   Mary Van Rensselaer Thayer, *Jacqueline Kennedy: The White House Years* (Boston: Little, Brown and Company, 1971), 112.

2   Ibid., 36.

3   Jacqueline Kennedy to J. B. West, undated. The White House.

4   Diana Vreeland, *D.V.* (New York: Alfred A. Knopf, 1984), 173.

CHAPTER SIXTEEN

[1] Mary Van Rensselaer Thayer, *Jacqueline Kennedy: The White House Years* (Boston: Little, Brown and Company, 1971), 135.

[2] Jansen, "Notes Concerning the White House," 14 February 1963. Private collection

[3] J. B. West, *Upstairs at the White House: My Life with the First Ladies* (New York: Coward, McCann & Geoghegan, 1973), 270.

[4] Jansen, Estimate No. 101.566, 1 May 1963. Private collection.

[5] Thayer, 135.

[6] Jansen, "Notes Concerning the White House," 14 February 1963. Private collection.

[7] William Voss Elder III to Jacqueline Kennedy, 18 September 1962. Private collection.

[8] West, 278.

[9] Thayer, 135.

[10] Ibid.

EPILOGUE

[1] "The White House Before the Kennedys and After . . . Now What?" *New York Times* Vol. 58 (July 27, 1970): 30.

[2] Jones designed the decorative schemes that replaced Boudin's White House work.

[3] William Seale, "Creating the Authentick Interior," *Historic Preservation Forum* Vol. 7, No. 6 (November/December 1993): 28.

[4] James Roe Ketchum to James Abbott, interview held in Washington, D.C., 29 May 1985.

[5] The Frenchman's textile documents for the Red Room are still being reproduced for the room. (Boudin's documented cerise-colored background was changed in 1972 to a more distinct red. At this time the all-silk body was changed to a silk and wool blend.) Fabrics he selected for the Green Room walls and the East Room draperies are still being used.

However, the Green Room moiré is now being manufactured by Scalamandré.

6   These figures were calculated from *The White House Collection, Preliminary Catalog of Furniture, Furnishings, Fine Arts and Documents, Acquired 1961–November 1964*. Winterthur Archives. Other statistics include nine beds, seven benches, twelve chests, seventeen desks, nineteen mirrors, seventeen settees and sofas, four sideboards, sixty-seven ceramic objects, twenty-six sets of fireplace tools, ten items of glassware, fifteen items of metalware, twenty textiles, and over two hundred items of fine art including paintings, sculpture, and works on paper.

Bibliography

Abbott, James A., and Elaine M. Rice. *A Frenchman in Camelot: The Decoration of the Kennedy White House by Stephane Boudin.* Cold Spring, New York: Boscobel Restoration, 1995.

Aikman, Lonnelle. *The Living White House.* 7th edition. Washington, D.C.: The White House Historical Association, 1982.

Ames, Kenneth L. Introduction, *The Colonial Revival in America,* Alan Axelrod, ed. New York: W. W. Norton & Company, 1985.

Burket, Harriet, ed. *House & Garden's Complete Guide to Interior Decoration.* New York: Bonanza Books, 1970.

Cantor, Jay E. *Winterthur.* New York: Harry N. Abrams, 1986.

Cassini, Oleg. *A Thousand Days of Magic: Dressing Jacqueline Kennedy for the White House.* New York: Rizzoli, 1995.

Cooper, Wendy A. *In Praise of America: American Decorative Arts, 1650–1830: Fifty Years of Discovery Since the 1929 Girl Scouts Loan Exhibition.* New York: Alfred A. Knopf, 1980.

Daniel, Jean Houston, and Price Daniel. *Executive Mansions and Capitols of America.* Waukesha, Wisconsin: Country Beautiful, 1969.

deFelice, Roger. *French Furniture Under Louis XVI and the Empire.* Translated by F. M. Atkinson. London: William Heinemann, 1920.

Garrett, Elisabeth, ed. *The Antiques Book of American Interiors: Colonial & Federal Styles.* New York: Harry N. Abrams, 1980.

Gere, Charlotte. *Nineteenth-Century Decoration: The Art of the Interior.* New York: Harry N. Abrams, 1989.

Hall, Gordon L., and Ann Pinchot. *Jacqueline Kennedy: A Biography.* New York: Frederick Fell, 1964.

Hampton, Mark. *Legendary Decorators of the Twentieth Century.* New York: Doubleday, 1992.

Harris, Neil. *Winterthur and America's Museum Age.* Winterthur, Delaware: The Henry Francis du Pont Winterthur Museum, 1981.

Heyman, C. David. *A Woman Named Jackie.* New York: Lyle Stuart, 1989.

Hosmer, Charles B., Jr. *Preservation Comes of Age.* Charlottesville, Virginia: University Press of Virginia, 1981.

—————. *Presence of the Past.* New York: G.P. Putnam's Sons, 1965.

Hunt-Jones, Conover. *Dolley and the "Great Little Madison."* Washington, D.C.: American Institute of Architects Foundation, 1977.

Johnson, Claudia [Lady Bird]. *A White House Diary.* New York: Holt, Rinehart and Winston, 1970.

Kunhardt, Philip B., Jr. *Life in Camelot: The Kennedy Years.* New York: Time, Inc., 1988.

Lincoln, Anne H. *The Kennedy White House Parties.* New York: Viking Press, 1967.

McConnell, Jane and Burt. *The White House: A History with Pictures.* New York: The Studio Publications, 1954.

Murtach, William J. *Keeping Time: The History and Theory of Preservation in America.* Pittstown, New Jersey: The Main Street Press, 1988.

Nylander, Richard C. *Wall Papers for Historic Buildings.* Washington, D.C.: The Preservation Press, 1983.

Praz, Mario. *An Illustrated History of Interior Decoration: From Pompeii to Art Nouveau.* New York: Thames and Hudson, 1982.

Rossano, Geoffrey L., ed. *Creating a Dignified Past: Museums and the Colonial Revival.* By Historic Cherry Hill. Savage, Maryland: Rowman and Littlefield Publishers, 1991.

Ryan, William, and Desmond Guinness. *The White House: An Architectural History.* New York: McGraw-Hill, 1980.

Schlesinger, Arthur, Jr. *A Thousand Days.* Boston: Little, Brown and Company, 1971.

Seale, William. *The President's House.* Washington, D.C.: The White House Historical Association, 1986.

————. *The White House: The History of an American Idea.* Washington, D.C.: The White House Historical Association, 1992.

Sorenson, Theodore. *Kennedy.* New York: Harper & Row, 1965.

Stillinger, Elizabeth. *The Antiquers.* New York: Alfred A. Knopf, 1980.

Sweeney, John A. H. *The Treasure House of Early American Rooms.* New York: Viking Press, 1963.

————. *Henry Francis du Pont 1880-1969.* Winterthur, Delaware: The Henry Francis du Pont Winterthur Museum, 1980.

————. *Winterthur Illustrated.* Winterthur, Delaware: The Henry Francis du Pont Winterthur Museum, 1963.

Thayer, Mary Van Rensselaer. *Jacqueline Kennedy: The White House Years.* Boston: Little, Brown and Company, 1971.

Thornton, Peter. *Authentic Decor: The Domestic Interior, 1620–1920.* New York: Viking, 1984.

Vreeland, Diana. *D.V.* Edited by George Plimpton. New York: Knopf, 1984.

Walker, John. *Self-Portrait with Donors: Confessions of an Art Collector.* Boston: Little Brown and Company, 1974.

West, James B. *Upstairs at the White House: My Life with the First Ladies.* New York: Coward, McCann and Geoghegan, 1973.

The White House Historical Association. *The White House: An Historic Guide.* 1st–15th editions. Washington, D.C.: The White House Historical Association, 1962–1982.

Willets, Gilson. *Inside History of the White House.* New York: The Christian Herald, 1908.

ARTICLES

Aikman, Lonnelle. "Inside the White House." *National Geographic* Vol. 119, No. 1 (January 1961): 2–43.

Alexander, Edward P. "Artistic and Historical Period Rooms." *Curator* Vol. VII, No. 4 (1964): 263–281.

Anthony, Carl Sferrazza. "Love, Jackie." *Forbes American Heritage* Vol. 45, No. 5 (September 1994): 90–100.

Berquist, Laura. "Life on the New Frontier." *Look* Vol. 26, No. 1 (January 1962): 16–29.

Brackner, Milton. "Parisian Assesses White House Decor." *New York Times* Vol. 49, 1 April 1961, sec 1.

Castro, Nash. "The Association's Twentieth Year." *White House History* Vol 1, No. 1 (1983): 22–27.

Cheshire, Maxine. "Circa 1962: Jacqueline Kennedy's White House." *Washington Post.* Series of eight articles appearing consecutively September 5–12, 1962.

Cornforth, John. "Boudin at Leeds Castle I." *Country Life* Vol. 1, No. 14 (April 1983): 925–928.

———. "Boudin at Leeds Castle II." *Country Life* Vol. 1, No. 21 (May 1983): 1018–1021.

Ditmer, Joanne. "White House Silk Designer." *Denver Post.* 4 December 1962: 27.

Filler, Martin. "A Clash of Tastes at the White House." *New York Times Magazine* (November 2, 1980): 82–108.

———. "Jackie, Queen of Arts." *House Beautiful* Vol. 136, No. 9 (September 1994): 90–93 and 146.

"A Flavor of History." *U.S. News and World Reports* Vol. LV, No. 23 (December 2, 1963): 12.

Gamarekian, Barbara. "A Curator's Philosophy: I Started the Hard Sell." *New York Times* Vol. 70, 10 November 1982, sec. M, II, 6.

Gould, Jack. "Mrs. Kennedy T.V. Hostess to the Nation." *New York Times.* 15 February 1962.

Hensley, Paul. "Henry Francis du Pont and the Williamsburg Connection." *Winterthur Newsletter* Vol. XXXII, No. 4 (Fall 1986): 5–6.

Jardel, Marguerite. "Tassinari and Châtel: 1762–1962." *La Revue Française* No. 137 (February 1962): supplement.

Kimball, Marie G. "The Original Furnishings of the White House, I." *The Magazine Antiques* Vol. XV, No. 6 (June 1929): 481–486.

———. "The Original Furnishings of the White House, II." *The Magazine Antiques* Vol. XVI, No.7 (July 1929): 33–37.

Montgomery, Charles F. "The First Ten Years of Winterthur as a Museum." *Winterthur Portfolio* Vol. I, (1964): 52–79.

"New Look in the White House." *Look* Vol. 26, No. 1 (January 2, 1962): 22–29.

Pearce, Lorraine Waxman. "Lannuier in the President's House." *The Magazine Antiques* Vol. LXXXI, No. 1 (January 1961): 94–96.

———. "American Empire Furniture in the White House." *The Magazine Antiques* Vol. LXXXI, No. 5 (May 1962): 515–519.

———. "Fine Federal Furniture in the White House." *The Magazine Antiques.* Vol. LXXXII, No. 3 (September 1962): 273–277.

"People." *Time* Vol. LXXVIII, No. 16 (October 20, 1961): 38.

Robertson, Nan. "Redecorated Red Room Has Colorful Debut at White House." *New York Times* Vol. 59, 9 November 1971.

Seale, William. "Creating the Authentick Interior." *Historic Preservation Forum* Vol. 7, No. 6 (November/December 1993): 27–36.

Sidey, Hugh. "The First Lady Brings History and Beauty to the White House." *Life* Vol. 51, No. 9 (September 6, 1961): 54–65.

Sweeney, John A. H. "The Evolution of the Winterthur Rooms." *Winterthur Portfolio* Vol. 1 (1964): 106–120.

"Toward the Ideal." *Time* Vol. 82, No. 10 (September 6, 1963): 60–67.

"The White House Before the Kennedys and After . . . Now What?" *New York Times* Vol. 58, 27 July 1970.

Winchester, Alice. Editorial. *The Magazine Antiques.* Vol. LXXI, No. 1 (January 1962): 85.

REPORTS

Castro, Nash. Minutes of meeting of Committee for the Preservation of the White House. White House, Washington, D.C., 17 February 1965. Mimeographed. The Lyndon B. Johnson Presidential Library, Austin, Texas.

Remarks of Mrs. Lyndon B. Johnson at a tea for members of the Fine Arts, Painting, and Advisory Committees on the Restoration of the White House. Delivered at the White House, Washington, D.C., 7 May 1964. Mimeographed. The Lyndon B. Johnson Presidential Library, Austin, Texas.

Report of the Commission on the Renovation of the Executive Mansion. Senator Kenneth D. McKellar, Chairman. Washington, D.C., 1952.

Report of the Committee for the Preservation of the White House, 1964–1969. George B. Hartzog, Jr., Chairman. Washington, D.C., 1968.

UNPUBLISHED WORKS

Abbott, James. "Restoration: Twenty-Five years of Interpretation." Bachelor's thesis, Vassar College, 1986.

Abbott, James. "A Frenchman in Camelot." Master's thesis, Fashion Institute of Technology/State University of New York, 1994.

Rice, Elaine M. "Furnishing Camelot: The Restoration of the White House Interiors 1961-1963, and the Role of H.F. duPont." Master's thesis, Winterthur Program in Early American Culture/The University of Delaware, 1993.

LETTERS

Bitter, Edwin, to James A. Abbott, Long Island City, New York, 15 September 1988.

Châtel, Jean-Jacques, to James A. Abbott, Paris, France, 12 October 1988.

Châtel, Jean-Jacques, to James A. Abbott, Paris, France, 20 May 1989.

Conger, Clement, to James A. Abbott, Washington, D.C. 13, March 1985.

du Pont, Henry Francis. Personal correspondence. Winterthur Archives, Winterthur, Delaware.

Elder, William Voss, III. Unpublished letters and communications to and from the White House Curator, June 1962–August 1963. Collection of William Voss Elder III.

Hampton, Mark, to James A. Abbott, New York, 13 January 1993.

Joseph Downs Manuscript and Microfilm Collection, Winterthur Museum. E.S. Yergason Scrapbook.

Pearce, Lorraine Waxman. Unpublished letters and communications. Collection of Lorraine Waxman Pearce.

Scalamandré, Franco. Unpublished letters and communications to and from the textile manufacturer, April 1960–September, 1971. Scalamandré Archives.

Van der Kemp, Gerald, to James A. Abbott, Giverny, France, 3 May 1987.

INTERVIEWS

Châtel, Jean-Jacques, to James Abbott, interview held at Tassinari and Châtel offices, Paris, France, 19 April 1988.

Conger, Clement, Curator of the White House to James Abbott, interview held at the Department of State, Washington, D.C., 30 May 1985.

du Pont, Henry Francis, to Harlan Phillips, transcript of interview for Archives of American Art, April 1962. Winterthur Archives.

Elder, William Voss, III, Curator Emeritus of the Baltimore Museum of Art, to James Abbott, interview held at Baltimore Museum of Art, Baltimore, Maryland 18 November 1992.

Elder, William Voss, III, to Elaine M. Rice, interview held at Baltimore Museum of Art, 12 March 1993.

Elder, William Voss, III, to Ronald H. Grele, transcript of interview for John F. Kennedy Library Oral History Project, December 15, 1965. Washington, D.C. William Voss Elder III, personal papers.

Hummel, Charles F., Curator Emeritus of Winterthur, to Elaine M. Rice, interview held at the Winterthur Museum, March 1993.

Ketchum, James Roe, Curator of the United States Senate, to James Abbott, interview held at the U.S. Capitol, Washington, D.C. 29 May 1985.

Levy, Bernard, to Elaine M. Rice, interview held at Bernard and S. Dean Levy, Inc., New York, 25 November 1992.

Pearce, Lorraine Waxman. Former Curator of the White House to Elaine Rice, interview held in Washington, D.C., 5 February 1993.

Lorraine Waxman Pearce, transcript of interview for "The World of Jacqueline Kennedy," 4 March 1962. Transcript, Lorraine Waxman Pearce personal collection.

Sweeney, John A. H. Curator Emeritus of Winterthur, to James Abbott, interview held at Philipsburg Manor, North Tarrytown, New York, April 1987.

Sweeney, John A. H. to Elaine M. Rice, Numerous interviews held at Winterthur Museum, Winterthur, Delaware, from September 1992 through the present.

Stockwell, David, to Elaine M. Rice, telephone interview, 18 March 1993.

Index